JAPANESE HOUSES

JAPANESE HOUSES
Patterns for Living

BY KIYOYUKI NISHIHARA

TRANSLATED BY RICHARD L. GAGE

JAPAN PUBLICATIONS, INC., TOKYO

Published by
Japan Publications, Inc., Tokyo

Distributed by
Japan Publications Trading Company
1255 Howard St., San Francisco, Calif. 94103
175 Fifth Ave., New York, N.Y. 10010
Central P.O. Box 722, Tokyo

Library of Congress Catalog Card No. 66–22390

First printing: January 1968

PRINTED IN JAPAN

PREFACE

An object's form contains its personality. The form of a thing both reflects the thoughts of the person who made it and expresses the individual personality of a people.

Curved lines that appear in traditional Japanese architecture are clearly different from those used in Western architecture because the cultural prototypes and the essential conceptual qualities of the two differ. Though this difference is not always apparent on the surface, I believe that we can see it clearly if we examine the process by which the given object itself was created.

Natural laws do not change from East to West, and the people in both realms, when confronted with the same conditions, make the same kinds of interpretations. If we examine in detail the methods and techniques used in certain situations, we can uncover the differences between the Oriental and Occidental thought processes. To make a curved line, the Japanese people apply very simple natural laws by curving a piece of string or bending a strip of wood into the desired shape. Westerners, on the other hand, use compass and protractor and apply geometric principles. If we are to understand the conceptual difference between the two kinds of curves, we must first grasp the difference in the processes by which they are obtained.

Using the Japanese method that relies on perception and intuition, one always requires the same set of circumstances to reproduce a given effect, whereas, with the Western method, as long as the theory remains unaltered, the identical effect is possible under any number of sets of circumstances.

If deducing general concepts from an analysis of psychological makeup is a permissible approach to clearly establishing the essential quality of a material culture, perhaps we can inversely demonstrate conceptual methodology by detailed analyses of the tools and methods used in the production of articles of a material culture. Let us use this way to indicate the differences between what we could call the Japanese approach and the Western approach.

Although the Japanese house grew out of a unique concept, the finished form alone without people in it looks like a cast-off shell, because it is the human life concealed within a house that gives it its life.

In writing about the Japanese house, I have placed great importance on human life. In part one, I have attempted to plumb

5

the process that created the Japanese psychological makeup and the Japanese attitude toward the house. In part two, I discuss the ways this attitude reflects in visual forms. In part three I explain the various characteristics of the Japanese house as I compare them with those of Western houses. In part four, while analyzing the elements that make up these characteristic features, I also discuss, one by one, all of the materials used in Japanese houses, and finally, in part five, I touch on ways to make good use of our traditional residential patterns in modern Japanese life and mention how these patterns are now changing.

Despite movements to actively preserve Japanese traditional culture, a great deal of the nation is being rebuilt through the important influence of rationalistic thought, because traditional methods often contradict the facts of modern life. Though the combination of traditional and modern Western may seem very strange to someone from another land, we Japanese are not conscious of confusion in the blend, because the visual disorder does not connect directly with the content of the building or of the city.

I will have achieved my goal if in this book I am able to prove that we should not look at a form through that form alone, and I will be pleased if in discussing Japanese houses as a way of life I can promote a further understanding of even one facet of Japanese culture.

Tokyo
September, 1967

Kiyoyuki Nishihara

ACKNOWLEDGMENTS

I should like to take this opportunity to express my deep gratitude to the following people, without whose help this book would not have seen the light of day.

For permitting us to photograph their houses:

Shirō Yamanari

Hajime Shimizu

Kinu Kameda

For permitting us to use their photographs:

Kiyotada Itō

The Sekai Bunka Co. (Tōkyō)

The Nihon Kenchiku Kyōkai (Ōsaka)

The Shōkoku Co. (Tōkyō)

The Imperial Household Agency

The Nara National Cultural Properties Research Laboratory, The Committee for the Preservation of Cultural Properties

The Tōkyō National Museum

Yukio Futagawa

Takeji Iwamiya

Fumio Murasawa

And to many other people who contributed photographs and whose names space limitations forbid me to include.

I should also like to thank all those authors who permitted me to use their texts, charts, and photographs.

I am very grateful to Iwao Yoshizaki of the Japan Publications, Inc., to Yukishige Takahashi who edited and put the book into form and saw it through production, and to Richard L. Gage who labored with the difficulties of rendering Japanese into English. Without all their help the project would never have seen a successful conclusion.

CONTENTS

9 CONTENTS

LIST OF ILLUSTRATIONS

13 LIST OF ILLUSTRATIONS

14 LIST OF ILLUSTRATIONS

17 LIST OF ILLUSTRATIONS

part one
THE ROOTS

1. NATURAL CONDITIONS AND ATTITUDES TOWARD LIFE

Of the peoples inhabiting this globe there are those whose natural environments are identical but whose attitudes towards daily living are completely dissimilar. Conversely, other groups, whose natural environments differ completely share common ideas about daily life. Although no rhyme or reason seems to govern these disparities, I believe that a closer examination will reveal some clues.

1. Points in Common

There is an objective rule, that we might call knowledge, common to all peoples in cases where various races have the same attitude toward life though their natural environments differ each from the other. Such knowledge is universal and transcends period and region. For instance, in the Swiss mountains the people build near their farmhouses log huts raised four or five feet above the ground on wooden posts. Below the huts between the supporting posts are flat dish-shaped stones put there to keep the rats from climbing to the floor above. Farmhouses in Northern Europe have similar huts, and we can find plenty of almost identical structures in Southeast Asia and Japan. It would be unnatural to assume that in some distant past era cultural exchange had existed between the Swiss mountains and Southeast Asia; moreover, the climate and topography of the two areas are totally different. Although certain common features exist between Switzerland and Northern Europe, neither is anything at all like Japan. The only possible similarities are the presence of timber in both areas and human inventiveness. We are forced to assume that the intervening something is a knowledge common to people everywhere.

Further substantiating this point is the similarity which noted German architect Bruno Taut pointed out between the farmhouses of the Sachsen-Anhalt region and those of Japan. The continued use, to the present, in this part of Germany of an ancient form in which the barn adjoins an earthern floored room is similar to the farmhouse type found in Northeastern Japan. In both versions the living and sleeping quarters are adjacent to and slightly elevated from the earthen-floored room, and in both the inhabitants observe the custom of removing shoes or wooden footwear before entering the elevated area. In some old Norwegian replicas we see houses with verandas on the south, just

21

1. The wooden posts of this farmhouse in the central mountainous region of Japan rise above a stone retaining wall. The horizontal members between the columns are for drying straw and other agricultural produce.

2. A farmhouse in the mountainous regions of northern Italy looks very much like its Japanese counterpart. The greatest similarity is more in the functionally identical drying racks than in the houses themselves.

(*right*)
3. An example of the ancient Japanese *azekura* style. As residential-compound granaries this architectural type dates back 2,000 years to the era in which Japanese culture was just budding. This particular example, the famous Shōsōin treasury in the precincts of the Tōdai-ji in Nara, was built in the Nara period, 1,100 years ago.

4. The many buildings like this in the Swiss mountains that look just like and serve the same function as their Japanese cousins are fine examples of the way human intellect works the same under similar climatic conditions.

like those in Japan. Grass thatch, of course, occurs in countless examples even today in Norway, Denmark, and Belgium.

2. Distinguishing Points

By contrast, some groups of the same race, speaking the same language and living under the same natural conditions, have created house styles with absolutely nothing in common. For

22 THE ROOTS

instance, in Alberobello, in the south of Italy, the people pile up small stones to make a cone-shaped affair roughly 15 feet in diameter and 13 feet tall. They coat the outside with plaster and live in the cone's lower areas. The neighbor's house is the same, and his neighbor's and so on until, surprisingly, the entire village is built of the same kind of house from the same materials. When a new house goes up, it too follows the ancient building method. Cross a single mountain, however, and this much beloved style vanishes without a trace. Here we find only rows of run-of-the-mill white-plastered rectangular houses covered with reddish-brown tile roofs. Natural conditions and topography in southern Italy do not vary radically from one side of a mountain to another, and it is impossible to explain such a wide discrepancy in residential style solely on the basis of these two factors. We must suppose that, in instances like this, in addition to a knowledge common to all people, some other sort of rational judgement is at work.

In a belt throughout southern Portugal, all of the houses are of stone covered with pure white plaster. In some villages, however, the frames around the doors and windows are painted yellow, though the rest of the finishing is just like that everywhere else in the region. To this day, I do not know the reason for the yellow frames.

These two sets of diametrically opposed examples indicate that human dwellings are not always built on rational bases. When different races have different cultural patterns, it is natural that their concepts of the house should differ. On the other hand, when we deal with completely different attitudes toward the house within a single framework of religious and social ideas we are in the realm of the influence of intuitive response to such natural phenomena as sensibility and taste.

Although our homes are deeply connected with natural phenomena, a close examination of them also reveals certain elements common to all humanity and certain distinctive qualities possessed only by given groups. In handling the Japanese house, I have preferred to emphasize those characteristics peculiar to the people of Japan.

3. Topography and Climate

The Japanese people have created their own cultural sphere on the four main islands of the long and narrow Japanese archipelago, which though as archaeology proves, was once a part of the Asiatic continent, now has a climate and topography remarkably different from that of the mainland.

Japan is indeed an island country, but the general tendency is to exaggerate the influence of the seas on the Japanese climate, which is more continental than oceanic, particularly in the winter.

5. Islands in the Seto Inland Sea. Countless small islands line the shores of Japan. It was these islands that bred Japan's distinctive culture and that kept her suitably removed from other cultural spheres.

Although the geographical latitude to some extent determines temperature, because of the cold northwest seasonal winds blowing from the low-temperature interior of the Asian continent, the Japanese winter is comparatively cold. On the other hand, the Japanese summer is hotter than the summers of other countries on the same latitude. Cold winters and hot humid summers make the Japanese climate less pleasant than those of other similarly located areas.

Japan has one of the world's heaviest rainfalls, a yearly average of 1,770 milimeters, or from two to three times that of the temperate areas in Europe or North America. A great regional difference exists in the amounts of rainfall throughout the country. On the northernmost island of Hokkaidō, the average is only 1,000 milimeters a year, but it increases to 2,000 on the southernmost island of Kyūshū. This is not to say, however, that heavy rainfall means the same kind of rain each month for all areas. The kinds of rainfall fit into three categories: the rains of the so-called rainy season, typhoon rains, and seasonal percipitation. Kyūshū and the land around the Seto Inland Sea get a great deal of the rainy-season rains, whereas the southern-part of the island of Shikoku and the coast of the Japan Sea, the area east of the Kinki region, suffer most from the typhoons. Winter percipitation tends to concentrate on the coast of the Japan Sea, north of the Hokuriku region. Rainy-season, typhoon, and seasonal per-

10. Japan's geographical position.
Since northern Japan is on the same latitude with northern Italy and since the country stretches out as long as the East Coast of the United States or the general Mediterranean area, the differences in climate from north to south are quite marked.

11. The regions of Japan.

6. Blossoms.
Spring in Japan means the cherry blossoms. Overnight they burst into full bloom, and overnight they rain lightly on the ground, till every petal has fallen. Sudden blossoming beauty and a gentle falling away are principles of Japanese life.

7. Lakes.
Trees and stones and deep green moss press close around the shores of Japan's still, deep, clear lakes.

8. Mountains.
Among Japan's many mountains, Fuji, towering alone near the Pacific shore, is the highest peak in the land, but it is not its height that sets it apart in the Japanese heart. Capped with sparkling snow, its thrillingly beautiful unadorned silhouette symbolizes the Japanese spirit of aspiration.

9. Snow.
In winter, half of Japan is covered in moist, packed snow, though the rivers never freeze and birds and beasts rummage among the white fields for burried bits of still green grass and leaves.

27 NATURAL CONDITIONS

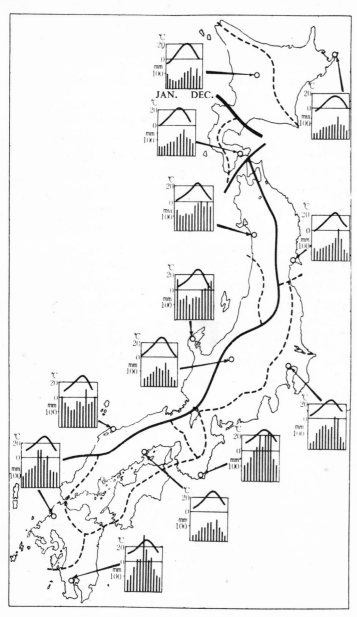

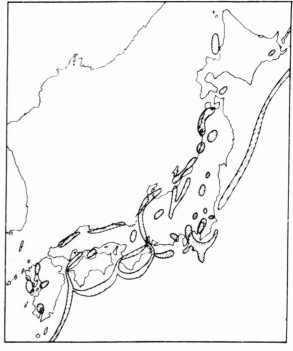

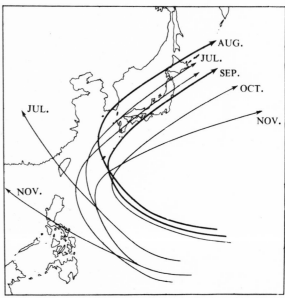

12. A climatic breakdown of the Japanese Islands. Not only do the northern and southern parts of the country have very different climates, the range of mountains running down the center of the archipelago results in pronounced climatic differences between the Pacific and the Sea of Japan coasts.

13. The earthquake belts.
The chart shows the areas that in the past have experienced record-setting earthquakes. Since the probability of more than one really violent tremor in the same locality is low, the number of Japanese people who in a lifetime experience a major quake is small, and the number who have experienced two is very small.

14. Seasonal alterations in typhoon paths.
Typhoons originating in the south seas and gradually moving north strike Japan usually at their peak forces. Heavy winds and rains most frequently hammer these islands in the so-called typhoon season, from the end of August through September.

cipitation greatly influence Japanese life in general, including Japanese houses.

The Japanese year is divided into four almost exactly equal seasons, but this does not, of course, mean that at the dividing point between two of them the weather radically changes. Because the country stretches 1,200 miles from the northeast to the southwest, when in March the northern Tōhoku region is still under a yard of snow, the southern tip of Kyūshū is enjoying the warmth of early summer. The seasonal changes tend to be earlier on the Pacific side than on the Japan Sea side of the islands.

In March, the buds begin to turn green, the peach and the peony bloom, and all of the flowers and grasses spring to life. At last, the pale cherry bursts into blossom as each spring rain brings warmer and warmer days. For centuries, the rich purple iris that bloom in May have symbolized the May fifth Boys' Day Festival. When May ends, so does spring, and the sultry, sweaty days increase in number. Summer lasts from June through August, but in June the effect of the monsoons bring on a long rainy season when the temperature and the humidity range in the seventies. This most characteristically Japanese of the seasons is a time when if one does not leave his house as open as possible, not only does it become impossible to remain in the muggy indoors, but foods, furniture, and clothing break out in a ghastly green mold. In mid-July, the rolling thunder drives away the rain and ushers in bright, hot summer. Great columns of billowing clouds march across a radiant blue sky from which blazes the golden sun. Autumn begins with the typhoons in September, but the heat of summer lingers on, and the humidity abates not a jot. Most of the typhoons, spawned in the Pacific, gradually increase in strength and speed as they approach the Japanese islands. Every year one or two lashing with raging winds and cutting rains strike crippling blows to the coastal areas. Once the storms are gone, however, the sky turns a deeper blue than ever, the air is crisp and dry, and true autumn, the most wonderful of the seasons, begins to flame with the gold of the gingko leaves and the crimson of the maples. In autumn blooms the giant chrysanthemum, second only to the cherry in the affections of the people. But the glory is brief, and with the falling of the last leaves, the winds of winter howl down from the north.

Winter lasts from December through February. Although snows blanket Hokkaidō, the Tōhoku district, and the areas along the Japan Sea, and fall from time to time elsewhere, despite fairly low temperatures, the warm rays of the sun do not weaken but keep things fairly warm—as long as the wind does not blow. When, in February, the dauntless plum braves the chill to bloom again, winter draws to a close, and the whole pageant renews itself with budding spring.

In general, the Japanese climate is hospitable to humanity. It lacks both hopeless, desolate stretches of desert and impenetrable tracks of jungle. Vegetation flourishes practically everywhere, and great ranges of forest make timber the most accessible material. Although Japan does not want for natural rock, it is deficient in easily processed sandstones and marbles.

The high temperatures and humidities of the Japanese summer caused the people to gradually develop an open-style house with deep protective eaves essential not only against long continuous rains and violent storms, but also as shade from the beating rays of the summer sun. Because the angle of the sun's radiation decreases in winter, the deep eaves still permit light to penetrate into the interiors. Wooden frames and clay walls prevent the formation of dew even when the moisture-laden spring and summer winds blow and cause rivulets of water to flow down stone and plaster walls, which though suitable to other areas, are ill at home in Japan. On the other hand, the deep eaves and open spaces are not always the best for Japan either. When the autumn typhoons rage, as they do at almost fixed times every year, the deeper the eaves the easier it is for the winds to lift off the roof. The more spacious the openings the weaker the structure and the likelier it is to collapse in the earthquakes that sometimes strike without warning.

Human rational judgement reflects strongly in the residence that represents both a solution to the problem of cold and to that of the peculiarly regional high winds, but the ancestors of the Japanese people, though doubtless they applied all of their knowledge, seem to have been unable to devise a house type that would suit all of the natural conditions of these islands.

Human nature is such that when we manage to fulfill one need, others sometimes go by the board. This means that we select one point on which to place most importance and more or less close our eyes to others. The method of assigning importance gives rise to judgement values that vary considerably. Although sometimes we inherit methods from people of other periods or follow customs established by tradition, certainly we often make decisions on the bases of personal feelings resulting from individual experience and personality.

An investigation of the Japanese house leads us to believe that the importance there falls on daily livability instead of on positive measures against such natural violence as typhoons and earthquakes. Every year, howling winds send many roofs flying and a large number of people lose their homes in torrential floods, but still the Japanese attitude remains one of harmonizing rather than opposing natural forces. When and why the Japanese people adopted this position will be the subject of our further discussion.

2. THE BIRTH OF THE HOUSE

1. *The House and Prayer*

Although it is uncertain when the present inhabitants of Japan came to live here, we know that roughly 10,000 years ago human beings dwelt in the Japanese archipelago because we have uncovered the remains of fires they used and some of their stone implements. Since, of course, no written records remain of those dim days, we can easily imagine that words themselves were then probably imperfect things. Without doubt, simply getting enough food to keep alive was a great difficulty, and even adequate places to sleep safe from wind and rain and wild beasts, impossible. How fearsome indeed must night have been! The great trees or deep caves where our ancestors saught safety were at best inadequate. Prayer was the only recourse. People then naturally wanted places where they could rest and eat, even or rainy days, or where untrembling they could enjoy the pleasures of the family circle in warmth, even in winter's biting cold. Things that we today take completely for granted presented to our forefathers problems urgently demanding solution. Providing themselves with a place that completely fulfilled even the simple function of shelter was beyond their powers. The less complete their shelter, the more their sense of security depended on prayers to some supernatural force. Houses were born under circumstances that tie them inseparably to prayers for safety.

2. *The Jōmon and Yayoi Cultures*

Roughly 10,000 years ago, in what geology calls the alluvial epoch, a new culture using earthen vessels and polished stone implements developed in Japan. This Jōmon culture, characterized by *jōmon* style pottery, so called because frequently the patterns on its surfaces were made by impressing rope into the clay, hence *jō* (rope) *mon* (decoration), spread throughout the country until the second or third centuries B.C., when the Yayoi culture began to replace it. The basic means of making a livelihood in the Jōmon was hunting the small beasts of the fields and mountains and the fish and shellfish of the sea. Cultivation of the land and cattle breeding had not yet appeared.

Because to scrape together enough food to live on the people had to work all day everyday, their living standards were low and their way of thinking primitive. They expressed their prayers in

15   16

17

15. Unglazed pottery jar some thousands of years old. Patterns made by impressing rope into the surface of the clay have given their name to the Jōmon period, the pottery of which such patterns characterize. The clay vessels of the period are generally thick and dark brown in color and feature a variety of ornamental devices. Since these vessels prevailed all over the country for several thousand years, forms and patterns vary considerably from district to district and from age to age.
Height: about two feet.
PROPERTY OF THE TŌKYŌ NATIONAL MUSEUM

16. Unglazed clay pot of the Yayoi period. In comparison with the pottery of the Jōmon period, that of the Yayoi period employs better quality clay, more advanced production methods, and higher firing temperatures. The finished ware is harder, the brighter colors are reddish brown or pale brown, and types and forms suit the purpose of the vessel. Produced in large quantities, the jars, pots, and jugs of this period are either simply ornamented or completely unadorned.
Height: about one foot.
PROPERTY OF THE TŌKYŌ NATIONAL MUSEUM

17. Unglazed pottery figure of the Jomon period. Though unable to draw the forms and lines of things themselves, the people of these distant days skilfully shaped representations of animals and humans in clay. Their primitive fantasy taught them that making and praying to figures like these would guarantee them easy delivery for their women and abundant wild game for food. In addition to clay figures, Jōmon people also made clay masks and stone figures in a rich array of types and styles, which altered more and more as time passed.
Height: about 10 inches.
PROPERTY OF THE TŌKYŌ NATIONAL MUSEUM

primitive baked pottery figures, many modeled after humans and animals but deformed by fearsome expressions and rendered in weird shapes. Not just Japan, but primitive societies in general have produced similar clay figures with exaggerated or abbreviated heads, hands, and feet, but the distinguishing point in the Jōmon figures is the presence on front and back of the same rope pattern that adorns Jōmon-period pottery vessels. From

32   THE ROOTS

the predominance in these figures of swelling exaggerated breasts and great bulging bellies we can assume that most of them represent a mother image. Not only from the positions and conditions in which these figures were excavated but also from their strange shapes we can easily imagine that they served some magical or religious purpose.

In about the second or third centuries B.C., during the Chinese Han dynasty,under a cultural stimulus from the Korean peninsula, a new culture arose in northern Kyūshū. Characterized by a more refined and advanced pottery than that of the Jōmon period, it is called the Yayoi culture. The presence in the bottoms of some Yayoi vessels of rice husks and the excavation of the remains of paddies and of various agricultural tools tell us that these people cultivated rice. They also used metal implements together with stone ones. The Yayoi culture extended to all corners of Japan by about the third century A.D.

The Yayoi people, who came from the continent and Korea, lead a psychologically quite different life from that of the Jōmon people. As tillers of the land instead of hunters and fishers they were more sensitive to nature. Cold, heat, long rains, the presence of water, drought, damage from insect, pests, fierce winds, all of these determined the abundance or dearth of the yearly rice crop. The Yayoi people considered natural phenomena acts of divinities with which the world of nature abounds, and they believed that if they worshipped these divinities and appeased their anger they could hope for protection from disaster and peace, abundant harvests, and prosperity.

3. *Idea and Art*

From the burial mounds, thought to have been erected from the third to the sixth century, together with such funerary objects as weapons, mirrors, and iron artifacts, have come a large number of *haniwa*, unglazed pottery figures ranging from simple cylinders to representations of houses, animals, coffins, ships, and humans. Figures of richly dressed ladies and of people playing musical instruments attest to the advanced character of the culture of the times. The ceramics techniques have clearly made rapid strides over those of earlier clay figures; moreover the *haniwa* fulfill the distinctly different purpose of offerings to the dead.

We must be careful to note, that both the older clay figures and the *haniwa* were not tools made directly to serve the purposes of human survival, with which their only connection, if they have one at all, lies in the birth of an art of prayer from the uncertainty which filled life and the home.

It seems likely that primitive people, lacking a script with which to write down thoughts, would turn to various clay vessels and clay figures to express their concepts. The very act of making

18. *Haniwa* figures.
Haniwa representations of human beings in many different sorts of clothing are a rich source of knowlege about ancient life in this country. Although the most usual figures are aristocrats or warriors in armor, we suppose that the ones in the photograph are farmers. They seem to represent the populace singing and dancing incantations for good harvests. Height: about two feet.
PROPERTY OF THE TŌKYŌ NATIONAL MUSUEM

19. Haniwa house.
Of the many non-human haniwa figures of animals, boats, etc., there are more than ten different kinds of houses. This one, dating from the fourth or fifth century B. C., is a gabled building with the entrance on the long side. Similar ridge covers, made of something that looks like wickerwork, are found in farm-houses even today.
PROPERTY OF THE TŌKYŌ NATIONAL MUSEUM

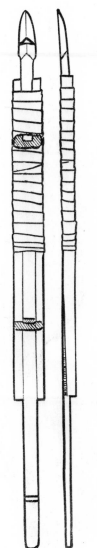

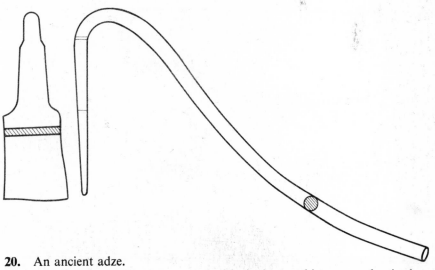

20. An ancient adze.
Probably the Japanese carpentry tool with the longest history, modernized versions of this old adze are used even today. The handle is wooden and the blade iron. You shave wood with it as you pull forward.

21. An ancient spear-plane.
A sharp piece of iron shaped like a spearhead is attached to two pieces of wood by a heavy cloth winding. To use the plane, the man of ages past held the cloth-wrapped section in his left hand and manipulated the blade as he would a knife by holding the long wooden section in his right hand.

35   THE BIRTH OF THE HOUSE

In addition to residing in specific stones and trees, divinities were thought to live in certain fixed areas called *shin'iki*. The rope (*shime-nawa*) and ritual paper folds (*shide*) indicated the place where the gods were believed to dwell.

the figures was a method of confirming their thoughts. We use letters and words to express our intentions, but our forefathers could do so only through objects made with clay. At the same time, *haniwa* and clay figures represent the most primitive form of art. Indeed they clearly demonstrate just how inseparably linked are human concepts and art.

4. The God Stone

Though the Japanese people loved the world of nature, in all its violent changes they found only one immutable object, stone, in which they could see both the shadow of the distant past and the symbol of things to come. They also believed that some specific stones, unlike all others, had the distinction of being divine. Though we can find god stones in all parts of the country, it is uncertain just when the idea of their divinity took root. Perhaps these stones performed a role similar to that of the clay figures which the people made and used to develop their thinking. The ancient Japanese thought with and used stones to nurture concepts.

Perhaps they first had an image of the existence of a divinity when they imagined that divinity to reside in stones. The clay figure was no longer a lump of clay but a work of the product of, a human process and of human hands, but the god stone was a divinity in unchanged natural form. It may be that the very reason for the stones' divinity was the fact that no human hand had ever done anything to them. Though it involves no conscious deeds, endowing these stones with sanctity is no less a positive human act than pouring prayers into the creation of clay figures. Herbert Reed says that the icon existed before the idea. When the ancient people of Japan first perceived divinity in stones they doubtless felt that they had for the first time given form, through action, to one of their own concepts.

5. Two Culture Currents

Primitive clay figures and the god stone clearly represent two opposed concepts. Though the relationship between the two lacks a well-defined historical explanation, perhaps we can find a clue in the notion that the former are thought to have come into this country from the southern districts and the latter from the north.

The process of overlaying northern shamanism on southern animism is the generally accepted prototype of Japanese culture. Southern cultural systems believe in many natural divinities—anima—which govern nature. These divinities dwell in the mountains, hills, valleys, and rivers and move abroad on a horizontal level. That is, rather than descending from the heavens, the anima are thought to leave the depths of the earth and the bottom of the sea and present themselves in strange masks and disguises. In contrast to this, northern shamanism, as expressed in mythology in the languages of the Altaic group, believes in divinities and ancestor spirits, who reside in lofty straight rising trees, and in evil spirits, who live under the earth. Under special conditions the shaman, and only he, using virgins as mediators, can communicate with the spirit world and sometimes divine secrets and prophesy the future. The practices are comparable in some respects to those of mediums in the West.

In Japanese religion, a combination of animism and shamanism, the lack of religious images is highly important. Rather than use intensified religious symbols, the Japanese prefer to see the gods as existing in nature itself. Since the gods live in the stones and the trees, it is no wonder that the Japanese desired to protect nature and to set a part of it aside so as to bring the divinity into their own immediate surroundings. Rather than rely on concrete representations and fixed images they preferred the mediation of a symbol and the unlimited power of fancy.

6. The Dwelling of the God

In the Ise Shrine, the oldest of all Japanese shrines, the object of worship is not a representation of a god, but a single ancient mirror. Although this mirror is the symbol of the god, its significance pales before that of the building that contains it. The gods do not transfer their divinity to images. They are everywhere near human beings, but since the human eye cannot detect them, the Japanese people placed their emphasis on the building in which the god was thought to reside. The elevated position high off the ground of the shrines in which the gods live in Japan proves a connection with Ural-Altaic mythology, in which the gods were believed to dwell in high places. Since the shamanistic gods are actually the ancestors of the people, the shrine in which they dwell takes its form from the extremely common grain storehouse. In other words, the makeup of the houses of the gods does not differ greatly from the makeup of the houses of the people.

Investigation into earlier Japanese society has failed to turn up evidence of shrine styles older than Ise. The tradition of completely rebuilding the Ise Shrine every 20 years is said to have begun in about 800 A.D. Although the reasons behind this transferral of the divinity dwelling from one site to a neighboring one are not very clear, before the development of shrine buildings, the gods would descend to a sanctified spot where the people, who were watching for it, could worship. This spot was by no means, however, the constant abiding place of the divinity in question. Perhaps the belief in gods who moved from place to place carried over, in the form of the ceremony of changing the

23. Ritual paper folds.
The paper in the *shide*, the ritual ornaments that mark the dwelling places of divinities, is the same white Japanese paper used for wrapping and letters. Practically anyone in Japan knows how to make *shide*. The rope into which the *shide* are stuck is made of straw.

dwelling of the god, into the age when buildings were used for worship.

If in ancient times the divinity had no permanent shrine, where did he abide? In all likelihood in what is called a *shin'iki*, or holy area, where the gods alone enter and no human can go. A rope (*shimenawa*) and paper ritual ornaments (*shide*) indicate the holy place which is sacred precisely because it is pristine nature with no traces of human planning or interference. The people believed that it was possible to transfer the divine spirit from the sacred grove to the shrine.

7. The Shrine

The shrine was deeply connected with the daily life of the people. They would go there to pray at the beginning of a new year or in times of birth, but they would also turn their steps there in attempts to appease the violent forces of earthquake, typhoon, flood, and fire when nature threatened havoc on even the guiltless. Unlike Christianity, this Japanese religion was not philanthropic. It developed rather from the practical need for safety against the vicissitudes of heaven and earth.

Places of worship could take the forms of small shrines in the corners of rice paddies, or lonely little buildings by the sides of roads. Sometimes they are either small buildings under large trees by the road, or great shrines deep in forest thickets. It is completely ordinary for them to appear in ravines, deep in mountain deeps, in caves on the seashore, or on lofty peaks.

Frequently, despite prayers for the protection of mystical natural powers, the supply of natural products from a certain area would stop. To prevent this, at the end of the hot humid summer when the time of harvests arrived, the people would hold a festival to express their gratitude to the gods. Bustling activity would invade the usually hushed shrine precincts. The people would build temporary huts of logs and bamboo in which to perform sacred dances and music. Through all the streets and lanes of the towns would jostle groups bearing on their shoulders the palanquin containing the deity or pulling the festival floats. Both of these activities were favorites, and although I do not know when they first came into being, I am sure that their origins date back many centuries. Even today in modern Tokyo similar crowds jog through the streets carrying the palanquin on festival occasions.

Although many Japanese people know of the dates of shrine festivals, the majority have no idea what deity the festivals celebrate or the circumstances under which that deity protects human beings. Their religion lacked holy writings, and theological questions did not bother the early Japanese. The very words *kami* (god) or *rei* (spirit) seem to have indicated centers of dif-

ferent powers which fulfilled wishes in response to prayers. The variety of gods assumed a variety of forms, had various characteristics, and resided in different shrines. This in itself should make it easy to see why the Japanese people used no images of their gods. They had no need for forms or images born of human imagination to represent forces that lived in shrines.

8.   The Pit-house and the Pile-house

Primitive Japanese dwellings appear clearly depicted in two types in relief on bronze mirrors excavated from the ancient burial mounds in Nara Prefecture. The first type is the *tate-ana* or pit-dwelling, and the second the *taka-yuka* or the pile-dwelling. Remains of *tate-ana* houses have turned up all over Japan. They seem to have been in wide use from the Jōmon period (until the third and second centuries B.C.) and in the Yayoi period (from the third and second centuries B.C. until the third and fourth centuries A.D.). Since pit-dwellings are scarcely ideal for a country where the summers are hot and humid and where in the wet seasons waters quickly accumulate, we suppose them to have been brought in by peoples from northern areas. The presence of tribes in northern Asia who even today live in pit-houses similar to those of the Jōmon ones, has lead many historians to believe that the Japanese of that age were hunting tribes who migrated here from the north. Apparently even after these hunters came to another country to live, they made no effort to change their northland customs of daily life.

The pit dwelling consisted of a pit about 1.5 feet deep and about 15 or 20 feet in diameter. From four to six posts were sunk into the pit to serve as the frame for a conical grass-thatch roof. Excavations have brought to light some instances in which the houses had stone hearths. Although, naturally, since all of the upper parts were vegetable matter, no examples of the original pit-house remain, using the excavated parts of a few columns from one of them, architectural historian Masaru Sekino was able to reconstruct a pit-dwelling. Searching for a building with posts that would closely resemble his fragments, Sekino came upon a drawing in a book from the Edo period (1603–1867) of a sand-iron blast furnace in the Izumo region which met his requirements. Adding information from this book to the repre-

(*preceding page*)
24.   Reconstructions of Yayoi buildings. The pit dwelling and the storehouse raised on piles (foreground), reconstructed on the basis of a great deal of research evoke an image of what residential buildings in the Yayoi period (third or second century B.C. to third or fourth century A.D.) must have actually been like. The Toro Remains, Shizuoka Prefecture.

Once parts of these buildings were buried, clean sand and pure underground water prevented them from rotting, so that today they give us a concrete idea of the wooden residences of an ancient time.
(Sugihara, Sōsuke. *Toro Iseki*, Tōkyō, 1964, Chūōkōron Bijutsu Shuppan)

25.   A group of pit dwellings. Pit dwellings (*tate-ana jūkyo*) are always found in groups. These remains, dating from the mid-Jōmon period, include seven pit dwellings and two sets of holes that we suppose are from the columns of pile-dwellings (*taka-yuka*). The presence of a communal trash dump prompts the notion that a group of families lead a community life here.

26. Simplified renditions of the houses from the back of the bronze mirror in figure 27.

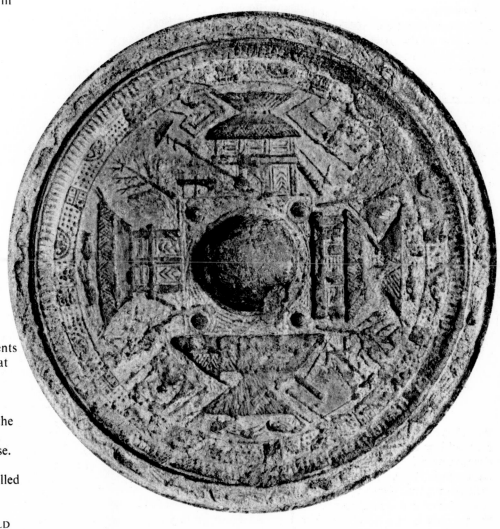

27. Bronze mirror (fourth century A.D.) with pictures of buildings on the back. The upper building represents the luxurious dwelling of an aristocrat of high station. It has a raised floor with a ladder in front and a sort of veranda. On the right is an ordinary house built on ground level and on the left an elevated-floor building with a ladder which is probably a storehouse. The bottom house is a commoner's pit dwelling. This mirror is the so-called house-picture mirror.
Diameter: about nine inches.
PROPERTY OF THE IMPERIAL HOUSEHOLD AGENCY

sentations of pit-dwellings found on the bronze bells and mirrors of the age of the burial mounds, he completed a reconstruction of a pit-house on the site of ancient remains in Toro, Shizuoka Prefecture. The building is now on public display.

Later, the supposition arose that perhaps in the center of the groups of pit-dwellings had stood another building of completely different structural type. Using the reliques of the lower parts of some posts, of a wooden step ladder, and of a sort of baseboard used to keep out rats as hints, researchers reached the conclusion that they were dealing with a storehouse raised off the ground on

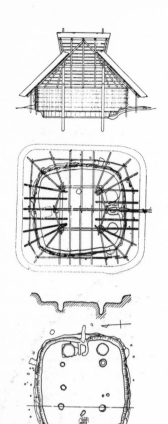

pilings. We believe that the agricultural peoples who came to Japan from the south introduced this building style because similar houses are in use today in parts of Southeast Asia. The use of an elevated floor in storehouses and its absence in residences is easily explained by the presence of a hearth for cooking in the latter and its absence in the former. As garners, these elevated buildings were certainly the most important in the village.

The general types, pit-house and pile-house, became the two main historical currents of Japanese houses. The pit-house became the rural village house and grew together with the common people, whereas the pile-house became the exclusive property of the ruling classes, the home of the aristocracy.

28. The plan of an excavated pit-dwelling shows four post holes and a hearth. On the basis of the relief on the bronze mirror back shown in figure 27 and the construction method in figure 31 we may imagine that the upper-section structure was as the chart shows it.

29. 30. Reconstruction based on the charts in figure 28.

31. The *tatara* hut. One of the fundamental pieces of information concerning the architectural structures of pit dwellings and one of the keys to their successful reconstruction was the *tatara* hut, a small building used to house a hearth for smelting iron. The architectural structures of the *tatara* huts seem to have been in use in the Jōmon and Yayoi periods and down into even later primitive times, but they vanished later.
(Sekino, Masaru. *Nihon Jūtaku Shōshi*, Tōkyō, 1960.)

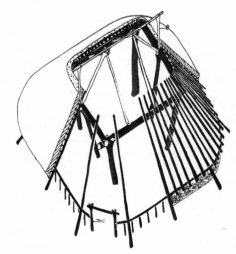

44   THE ROOTS

9. Two Development Currents

Recently Hirotarō Ota of Tokyo University has published an interesting theory, which, though not without dubious points in methodology, deserves praise above scholastic considerations for the boldness of its thought. I should like to discuss it briefly.

Ota believes that perhaps the pile-house, instead of originating as a storehouse, served as a dwelling from its earliest days. He uses as his demonstration the houses of underdeveloped areas in the South Pacific today and the Japanese house of the middle ages, and his chief selling point is the hearth.

The presence of the hearth for cooking in the middle of the pit-dwelling clearly points out the building's residential function, but it is possible to conceive of a pile-house in which the cooking was done in a separate building. Indeed examples of this arrangement exist.

The next point of attention is the roof framework method. Japanese urban houses, whether their roof is gabled (*kirizuma*) or hipped (*yosemune*) in style, use the same framework method, the so-called Japanese truss (*wa-goya*). This system employs cross-beams that rest on posts. Short posts resting on the crossbeams support the roof. Instead of this system, however, farmhouses use slanting main members arranged in an inverted V *gasshō* roof. The difference in roof structure became traditional in ancient times.

The very Japanese word for gabled roof (*kirizuma*) connotes the main structural system and *yosemune* or hipped roof indicates a rural-style construction, probably because the gabled roof demanded more technical skill than the hipped roof. The tendency to regard the gabled roof as somehow superior continued until the importation of Buddhist architecture. It is easy to understand why practically all Japanese shrines use gabled roofs.

A difference in the placement of the rafters also exists between the two roof types. In the gabled roof rafters run parallel, but in the hipped roof they are radially arranged. Because parallel rafters must result in a rectangular floor plan, but radial ones naturally permit roundness, pit-dwellings have rounded floor plans.

Ota classifies Japanese dwellings into two systems on the basis of the above considerations:

1. Pile-house: gabled roof, (post frame), parallel rafters, cooking in a separate building—brought into Japan from the south.
2. Pit-house: hipped roof (inverted-V frame), radially arranged rafters, cooking inside the building—brought into Japan from the north.

The former came down in history as the house of the aristocrats, whereas the latter remained the house of the common people, though it did later acquire flooring as a result of the influence of the homes of the upper classes.

3. THE HOUSE AND FAMILY MAKEUP

1. From Family to Tribe

Gradually in the Jōmon period, the sizes of the settlements of pit-dwellings increased. From the horseshoe shape and the plaza-like opening in the settlements uncovered near Tōkyō and from the fixed locations of the trash dumps we suppose that already in those times the people observed some social order. The communal burial grounds found with the village remains in the Okayama Prefecture area indicate the growth of the primitive settlement into a unit that remained in use for a number of generations. Some hold that the process of creating these settlements moved from one of strictly family relations (father, mother, and children), to one of kin (immediate family, grandparents, and younger cousins, etc.), to one of clan (an aggregation of people with family connections that extend over several generations). Some scholars hold that at this same time the practice arose of marrying a group of young people of a single generation from one settlement to a group of people of one generation from another settlement. The system is similar to the punalua common from Melanesia to New Guinea. In a punalua, the men marry into the houses of the women, where the children are raised, thus increasing the power of female authority and creating a matriarchal family. Doubtless, in areas where this system prevails, women are often tribal chiefs. Though the group marriage in Japan continued as long as hunting and foraging were the main ways of obtaining food, with the introduction of rice cultivation and as the role of male labor increased in importance, demands for a more individual form of married life caused the older system to naturally fade out. Once the marriage system becomes individualized, the male tends to assume a more authoritative role. For this reason, as the primitive communal society moved toward a clan structure, the ancient *kuni*, or domains, came into being, and the family became patriarchal.

2. The Continental Influence

In the sixth century A.D., Japan for the first time came into contact with a great foreign culture. The vast scale and venerable age of the Chinese giant caused the ancient Japanese no small amount of anxiety and agitation, because compared with the Chinese the culture of Japan was small in scale and ideologically

46

shallow. It lacked even a written language. China, on the other hand, could boast a philosophy and ideology dating back several thousands of years.

Probably one of the greatest blows to the Japanese was the complete absence of any written history of their country. Without a written language they could rely only on tales and word of mouth; scholarly history was beyond them. The first written history of Japan, the *Kojiki*, or Record of Ancient Matters, is written in Chinese characters. Naturally, with written language, the Japanese also imported scholarly learning and thought.

Compared with the extravagant free imaginative powers of the Chinese, the ancient Japanese, though artistic, were technically immature. Absorbing and digesting the culture of their neighbor was as big a task as they could handle. Ancient Japan, like ancient Greece, lacked the sort of architectural styles the Chinese used, in which magnificence overpowers and inspires a silent sense of awe, a feeling particularly useful to ruling classes in managing underlings. Quite naturally, as Chinese culture swept into this country, the Japanese nobility recognized the political advantages of ostentation, and their homes assumed an exaggerated grandeur. Simultaneously with advanced techniques and thought, the Japanese also imported architectural styles to show off the majesty and might of the aristocrats. This whole-hearted liking for the continental on the part of the rulers did not go completely uncriticized; in fact, it met with much tacit resistance.

3. Aristocrats and Commoners

In the *Nenjū Gyōji* (Annual Rites and Ceremonies) scroll of the twelfth century we see pictured representations of homes of both the aristocrats and of the commoners of those times.

The wealthy lived in mansions built in what is called the *shinden* style, which originally called for complete left-right symmetry, but which in this country became asymmetrical shortly after its importation. In general, a *shinden* home would occupy a site of about five acres. Facing south on the site would stand the *seiden*, or main hall, to the east, west, northeast, and northwest of which were outbuildings called *tai-no-ya*. Covered corridors connected all of the buildings. In the southern tip of the site at the end of a corridor leading from one of the *tai-no-ya* was a pavilion called the *tsuridono*, under which streams were frequently directed or springs caused to bubble up. Around the outsides of each of the buildings ran verandas with open plank flooring and sometimes with handrails. The roof was usually covered in cypress shingles. The floor, raised a few feet from the ground, was planked, and the supporting columns are said to have, in some instances, reached diameters of one foot.

47 THE HOUSE AND FAMILY MAKEUP

32. The *shinden* style.
A home of an aristocrat of ancient times. (*Nenjū Gyōji* scrolls)

34. Commoners' houses of the eleventh and twelfth centuries.
These pictures of life in the Kyoto of the period show houses lined in a row with one third of the frontage given over to entrance. The remaining two thirds were occupied by a board-floored area. Some of the buildings are shops with wares lined up sometimes between boards but most often on shelves attached to the windows. Almost all of the fronts are covered in either wickerwork or boards.

33. Interior of the residence of an aristocrat of the eleventh or twelfth century. This picture comes from volume 3 of the *Kasuga Gongen Genki* scrolls which relate, in 20 volumes, the origin of the famous Kasuga Shrine and various miraculous happenings that occurred there from 937 to 1304.

35. Farmhouse of around the tenth century. This picture is taken from volume 3 of the *Shigisan Engi* scrolls, which tell three tales of miracles connected with the tenth-century abbot Myōren of the temple Chōgosonshi-ji on Mt. Shigi, in Nara Prefecture. The scrolls are counted some of the finest Japanese works of the kind.

The master of the house both lived and conducted ceremonies and audiences in the *seiden*, while his family and attendants lived in the *tai-no-ya*. Aside from rooms for sleeping and storage, spaces were largely unpartitioned. Sliding paper-covered partitions (*fusuma*) and door-window panels (*shōji*) had not yet been invented. Instead of covering the entire floor with grass mats (*tatami*), as the Japanese later did, the aristocrats of ancient times used grass cushions called *okidatami* which they moved from place to place on the planked floor as was necessary. Single leaf screens, folding screens, and a cloth hung on a framework called a *kichō* served as partitions when needed, and sliding doors something like the later *fusuma* also divided spaces from one another.

The same *Nenjū Gyōji* scroll contains pictures of the homes of the commoners as well as of the nobility. Homes of the lowly, in contrast with those of the exalted, occupied little space. Narrow in frontage, but very deep, town houses jammed one against the other lined the streets of Heian-kyō, as Kyōto the capital was then called. Population growth and flourishing trade are doubtless responsible for the urban dwelling form and placement.

36. Home of a warrior of the Kamakura period (1192–1333).
Warriors' houses of the period stood on high hills where they had views of the entire village or by main arteries of transportation. Since the warriors managed the district in which they lived, their houses were somewhat different from those of the generality. A moat and a board wall usually surrounded them, and spears and bows and arrows stood always in readiness. To the left of the main entrance was the master's dwelling. The interior had wooden floors with one section of *tatami*. Barns for horses were in separate buildings. On the whole, the house was a simple but relaxed affair. (From the *Hōnen Shōnin* scrolls)

37. Home of a warrior of the same period.
The master, seated on *tatami* spread on a board floor, receives a guest. The picture shows a guest of low station who had to go around by the veranda and address the lord without actually entering the house. Sliding doors were not yet common, and this house still uses the *shitomido* that is lifted and hooked up from above. (From the the *Hōnen Shōnin* scrolls)

Most of the houses in the scroll have a frontage of about 12 or 18 feet. We imagine that all their depths were about the same. The front is usually divided into three sections: one third for the entrance, and the other two thirds for windows. Since the room nearest the entrance does not seem to be a sleeping area, even then, the interior may have been vaguely divided into living room and sleeping room.

The townhouse from the Heian period into the middle ages resembles the farmhouse of the times in that part of the interior is earthen floored and part floored with boards. The board floored area is further divided into living and sleeping quarters. The upper part of the front wall would have high windows fitted with wooden lattices that opened upward. The lower section of the wall would be either basket-woven bamboo (*ajiro*) or clay. The door was made of planks, and the same material served as roofing. Deep eaves shaded both the front and back of the house. Interior fittings included sliding doors and something that resembled *shōji*. By contrast with the homes of the aristocrats, the commoner's dwelling showed practically no continental influence.

4. *Growing Restrictions from Above and Below*

Skipping over the centuries to the Edo period (1603–1867), we find Japan in the grips of the Tokugawa shogunate. Because it feared any strengthening of the people's economic powers, the government adopted a policy of such burdensome levies on the farmers, that for these unfortunates merely to eat and have something to wear and some place to live required tremendous labor. To make things worse, when such disasters as the great Edo fire, in 1657, occurred, the government would take the chance to issue strict controls on the buildings of homes not only for the farmers but for the city folk as well. Controls extended to the sizes of entrances, the shapes of roofs, and the pictures one might paint on sliding paper doors. A great fire in Edo meant that it was economically difficult to rebuild resplendent mansions.

Nor did clothing escape the oppressive hand of the shogunate. Although village headmen and other officials might wear silk, the general citizenry, both rural and urban, had to content itself with patternless black or indigo cotton or linen. Sleeve lengths, too, were perscribed.

The social makeup of the village of the Edo period consisted of the owner of the land, who bore the heavy burden of paying the yearly tribute in kind, in other words the true farmers, and a second class of agricultural workers who were actually no more than tenants. Since the farm work demanded a constantly stable supply of labor, powerful restrictions grew up to prevent parcelling of the land. Under these restrictions children and grand-

38. Farmhouse of the early Edo period.
As the tile techniques gradually spread to domestic architecture, straw and bark-shingle roofs declined.
Walls, too, gradually changed from mere mud plaster to pure white plaster. The Yoshimura house, remaining intact from the seventeenth century, is one of the few examples we have of the almost complete Japanese farmhouse style. The government has designated it a national treasure.

children had to bring their new wives into a compound family system that tended to continue and grow more tenacious. In 1673, to maintain the level of agricultural production by preventing the farmers from creating minimal holdings, the government forbade the sale of arable lands. Since agricultural production was already low, any further reduction in field size by sale would spell the downfall of both the buyer and of the original owner. On the other hand, though it might amount to little, any increase in agricultural production power caused growth in the cities, the consumer markets. An increased demand for labor in the cities inevitably lured the villagers away from the detested farm drudgery. Urban flight of farm labor dealt the farmers a serious blow. Since they were faced with this problem on the one hand and with the grasping of the ruling classes on the other, to assure that they produced the requisite amount, the independent farmers moved more and more to the compound family system in which the young husband brought his new bride into the home to be a helping hand. However, the shogunate's ban on land division and sale prompted a rise in the amount of sharecropping.

In the mountain villages, where geography restricts the amount of arable land and makes even sharecropping difficult, the big family system has continued down into modern times. This is why the village of Shirakawa so well preserves the image of times gone. Up until the middle of the nineteenth century, in the village of Nakagiri, out of a total of 43 households, 28 housed from 10 to 20 people, and 10 actually housed more than 20 people. The second and third sons could not establish branch families, and the daughters were attached to the house to such an extent that they could not marry. All they could call their own was what they managed to scrape together in their few hours of leisure or on their holidays, and though a man might have children of his own, when he died, his possessions became the property of the head of the house. The governing privilege of the head of the house, even over those who had married, made privacy within the family impossible. If privacy is unessential to the people, what is the need of improving the methods used to partition the spaces in the house where the people live? The houses of Shirakawa village, use a large structural framework, and although the building techniques, in general, are advanced, the partitioning is crude. The very crudeness probably reflects a lack of interest in privacy.

In addition to tilling the land, the family also bred silkworms, and, of course, they had to have places to eat and sleep. But they did all of these things together so that functional divisions of the spaces, except for some partitioning in sleeping areas, were unnecessary. Even the sleeping areas sometimes had to serve as lofts for the silkworms. Naturally spaces were multi-purpose.

The situation in the cities was somewhat different, in that there the number of unmarried employees who dwelt in their master's

52 THE ROOTS

houses was greater than the number of family members who married and brought spouses in to live. In addition, a merchant of the city would also provide many of his workers' relatives with shelter, so that to make suitable provisions city houses lined along the streets were frequently very large. Establishing an independent household would present ordinary workers and relatives with almost insurmountable financial difficulties.

5. *Modern Japanese Houses*

Because the birth of Japan as a modern nation was extremely late the evolution of a family system centering on the married couple did not develop until the late nineteenth and early twentieth centuries, when, in the Meiji period, Western modern thought invaded these shores. In 300 years of isolation, Japanese culture pursued an almost too unique path of development so that when the great wave of Western influence began to break over her, the task of assimilation was very difficult. Then by then shaky

53 THE HOUSE AND FAMILY MAKEUP

39. A Meiji-period office.
By the mid-nineteenth century, when this building was built, tiles had become the ordinary roof for shops and offices as well as houses. This bank building is in a style that suggests the godowns used even today because they offer fire protection. The thick plastered walls are painted black in this case.

40. A Meiji residence.
Farmhouses gradually lost strict left-right symmetry till by the Meiji period we find something like this, a number of roofs joined together in a complicated pattern. The thin board covering on the house weathers a dark color, but the godown on the left preserves its sparkling white.

41. Another Meiji house

Tokugawa government was understandably very hesitant about adopting modern thought and doctrines of Christianity which threatened the foundations of its power. When the power passed from Tokugawa hands into those of the new power class, at practically one instant, new Western ideas flooded in to greatly alter Japanese daily life.

The most influential importations were modern thought and revolutions in production methods. The old social distinctions of samurai, farmer, craftsman, and tradesmen vanished before the legalized quarantee of equal rights to all people.

The formerly priviliged samurai class fell on evil days indeed. As the country imported lock stock and barrel the almost perfectly completed results of the Industrial Revolution, the Japanese production scale suddenly charged upward. Capital accumulation and the number of products on the marked followed suit, and the combination of modern thought and revolutionized production machinery gave rise to a social class new to the Japanese, the white-collar worker, or what is called in Japanese the salaryman (*sarariman*). The salaryman, the pillar of the family based on the married couple and children, resides in homes prepared by the capitalist class or by the government or in urban and suburban houses built by small and medium landowners for rent to countless anybodies.

Built for profit, these houses go into circulation as commercial items which sensitively reflect the people's feelings about life. They show what the ideal is, and that ideal, in this case, is the home of the former ruling-class samurai.

42. A Meiji store.
A liquor store facing a busy street, this shop boasts an eminently prominent beer advertisement. Beer itself was imported in those days from the West, but Western influence had not yet touched the building.

43. A second Meiji store.
Here is another liquor store, one that also features advertisements for wine and milk. The people inside are dressed in Western-style clothing, but the ones passing in front, with kimono and snappy Occidental headgear, give a real taste of Meiji atmosphere.

44. A third Meiji store.
This building clearly shows Western architectural influence in the balcony at the entrance and in the Western way of fitting windows. Like clothing, architecture too could be a blend of the traditions of home and abroad, as the Japanese-style tile inlay in the upper section of the building shows. A school of Western cooking, this unusual establishment also provided tables and equipment for those fond of billiards.

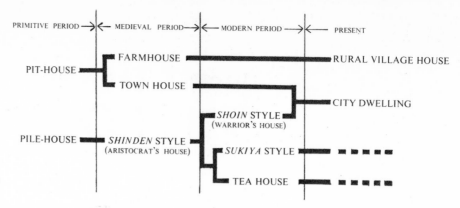

PRIMITIVE PERIOD → ← MEDIEVAL PERIOD → ← MODERN PERIOD → ← PRESENT

PIT-HOUSE

FARMHOUSE — RURAL VILLAGE HOUSE

TOWN HOUSE

SHOIN STYLE
(WARRIOR'S HOUSE) — CITY DWELLING

PILE-HOUSE — SHINDEN STYLE
(ARISTOCRAT'S HOUSE)

SUKIYA STYLE

TEA HOUSE

45. A style chart of Japanese houses.

6. *Today's Image of the House*

When the samurai class suffered dispersal, so that the common people came into closer contact with them, a new kind of private dwelling began to appear among the masses. Whatever the house, it was sure to have the kind of entrance hall (*genkan*) and sitting room with ornamental alcove (*tokonoma*) and shelves (*chigaidana*) that all samurai homes had featured. Also, as in samurai homes, these new dwellings would have small studies and a long corridor leading from the sitting room to the entranceway and opening on the south onto a small garden. Although these things were requisite features of a samurai house, as the urban population rapidly increased and housing became scarce, ease of construction and sale became the goal, and the scales of the houses gradually dwindled. Still the common people, so long under the thumbs of their rulers, were loath to abandon their aspirations for what had been samurai-like and tended to preserve in their homes the lifeless forms of bygone days. Of course, the tendency only invited vulgarity. Despite the establishment of a society in which the married couple and their children comprised the core, false samurai-style houses continued to be the rage even though they ignore the functional needs of everyday living. Even in the face of the influence of social and industrial revolution, however, the traditional Japanese partitioning pattern, in which *fusuma* provide only semi-separation of spaces, and the multi-purpose use of rooms remained unchanged to contradict the growing demand for individual privacy.

The basic change in the structure of the house came after the Second World War, when Western democracy swept into the country and toppled the father of the house from his position of absolute authority. Respect then developed for individual life within the home, and even children began to get their own private rooms. Once the family positions within the house were firmly established, for the first time, the kitchen, now the center of married life, shook off its traditional grime and gloom and became a bright cheery place. Once again, as throughout Japanese history, changes in family station and the prevalent family system play a very important part in the layout of the Japanese house.

part two
THE FORMS

4. THE RESIDENTIAL IMAGE

THERE are two kinds of residential pattern: the visual pattern made up of the things we can see and touch, and the activity pattern, including all family work and activity, individual or group, which is governed on the basis of hints taken from the visual pattern. In other words, humans build their houses to conform with their ways of living. Our custom of regarding a house as a piece of architecture runs completely counter to the basic nature of the house. The mere building is, in fact, no more than a shell. Although a house should be formed in size and divisions that suit the needs of its dwellers, with the birth of a class society and variations in income, lower-status families found themselves unable always to procure for their houses the amount of space they actually required. Growth of cities, traffic, and increases in urban density resulted in living conditions opposed to actual family needs. Consequently, people adopted the custom of making their living activities conform to the pattern of an already existing building. This meant that the visual pattern set the conditions for the activity pattern and gave rise to a split between the house as it should essentially be and ways of living, in other words, to a split between the visual and the activity patterns.

In the first part of the book I have already explained the roots of the Japanese house and the knowledge of life the Japanese people evolved from their natural setting. I should now like to turn to its visual image—its forms.

1. The Ground-breaking and Structure-raising Ceremonies

The distinctively Japanese faith Shintōism, though dear to most Japanese hearts, is often not called a true religion because the spirits it celebrates are not really gods. Every Japanese knows about Shintō, but practically none of them can accurately explain Shintō deities. Shintō is more an ideological culture, an art of life that serves to cultivate morality. White robed priests, folded paper ornaments (*shide*) woven into straw rope and symbolizing purity, and lengthy performances of dissonant music are all parts of Shintō ceremonies and festivals. The distinctive type of beauty apparent in Shintō forms agrees with the Japanese sense of life.

In accordance with Shintō traditions, any Japanese who decides to build, whether a small wooden house or a towering con-

59

46–54. Erecting the structure.
First the posts.
Then the beams.
Joining the beams.
More beams.
Temporary braces prevent the posts from inclining.

Putting the second-story posts in place.
Then the beams.
Correcting one of the joint holes.
The final touch—attaching to the ridge the paper talisman representing a prayer for the future safety of the house.

55. Even after the structure is up and the roof is on, the talisman remains. The writing on the column indicates that this is number seven column in the "*ho*" block of the grid, *ho* being simply one of the symbols in the Japanese syllabary.

61   THE RESIDENTIAL IMAGE

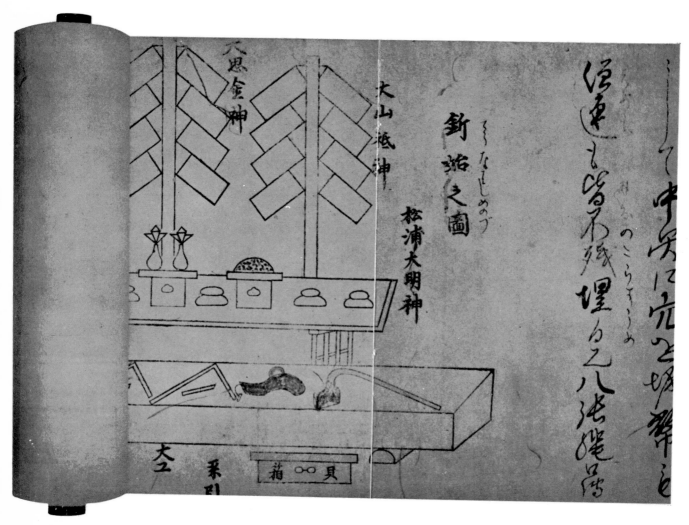

天恩金神

大山祇神

釿始之図

松浦大明神

しめのつ

56. Until the end of the eighteenth century, all of the tools used in building a house were brought together for a Shintō purification ceremony.

crete building will always think first of the essential ground breaking ceremony. In almost the dead center of the rolled site, they drive a stake. It is not clear whether this stake is intended to be a relic of the sacred *shin-no-mihashira* or whether it merely indicates the place on which the building will stand. Around the stake in a square will stand four bamboo poles with the leaves still on them. Generally, the rough square is about twelve feet to a side. From each of the poles, all around the square, is draped a straw rope with folded white paper ornaments woven into it. The rope and the ornaments designate the enclosed area as a sacred place. All these preparations set the stage for the solemn celebration of the ceremony. In the center of the square will stand a small altar on which are pure white porcelain vases filled with the leaves and branches of the *sakaki*, a tree sacred to Shintōism. Before these vases stand the offerings of rice, sake, vegetables, and fish, in variety and quantity according to the affluence of the man building the house.

At last the priest in pure white, or sometimes in gold and purple over white, and wearing a tall black woven horsehair hat and black lacquered wooden shoes of a particular kind, enters the grounds, and all the people standing around bow low to him. The priest reads the ritual (*norito*) then turns to the earth itself and addresses to it a long, low, humming recitation to invoke the god who will protect the house site. When the deity has been invited, it is safe to build a house on the land. The priest then turns to the four corners of the square and from a small box sprinkles bits of white paper and rice in each direction to symbolically drive out evil spirits. He again addresses himself to the earth in a low humming voice to ask the deity to return to its home. This concludes the ceremony.

All of the people attending then drink the god's sake from the altar, and construction can begin on the following day.

Once the ridge pole, the highest member of the structure, and all the basic structure of the house is finished, we hold another ceremony called the *tate-mae*. In Europe, a similar ceremony using a crown with colored streamers occurs, but here in Japan we use a small piece of wood on which are painted a number of black ink stripes and from which hangs a folded paper ornament similar to the *shide*. This is attached to the ridge pole. In some cases, to symbolically chase away evil spirits we also affix to the pole a fully drawn bow with an arrow fitted to the string. When the ceremony is over we take down the bow, but the painted wooden strip and its folded paper remain to be a constant prayer for the safety and protection of the house. Since preparatory cutting and fitting of the beams and columns are completed beforehand, it only takes one day to put everything up. As the sun sets on the day of the *tate-mae*, the owner of the house and the carpenters are able to sit under the completed structure, drink sake together, and sing songs in prayer for the success of the remaining construction work.

2. Time-honored Auguries

Divination exercises such strongly rooted controls over the building of houses in Japan that it is impossible to discard its regulations as mere superstition. Even today, many Japanese people, fully aware that they completely lack scientific grounds, rely on divination's methods. For instance, traditionally no Japanese house has an entrance on the northeast or a toilet or well on the southwest. Although we might find reasons for some of these tabus, the whole truth is that Chinese divination was incorporated into the Japanese system without regard for reason. True, in winter, the cold winds blow from the northeast making that a poor direction for an entrance way. True, in the hot summer, an old-fashioned toilet would smell foul and the water in a well might tend to sour in the hot southwestern sun. But the fact remains that not all of Japan's regions have the same climates. Why then should the rules for placement of parts of a house be

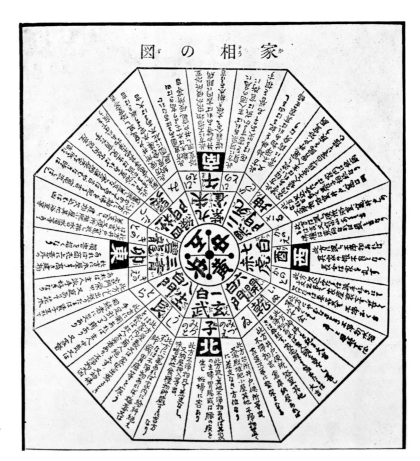

57. This chart foretells which directions, placements, and structures are propitious and which ill-omened in building a house. It tells us, for instance, that if the toilet, well, or bath should be on the south, the family will suffer from eye disease.

58. A divination almanac. Almanacs of this kind are published yearly even today. This page for September shows both solar and lunar calendars.

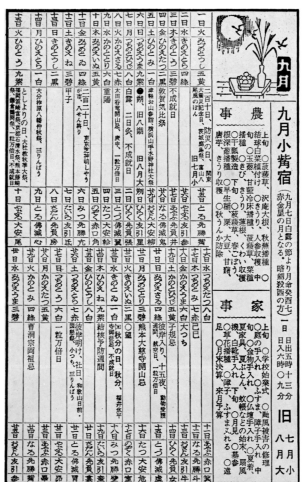

the same all over the country? Of the total of 24 such rules, some 2 or 3 have logical explanations in the light of Japanese climatic conditions, but many of them cannot be logically explained at all.

Divination's rules for selecting directions and for selecting days are deeply connected with the Japanese house. The direction of the house—and there are many more minute regulations like the ones we have just discussed—is called the *kaso*. The mystic rules for *kasō* divination are inscribed in an octagon divided into 24 segments. What is written in these segments are the basic elements of the divination. Using this together with the day, month, and year of the householder's birth, the diviner makes his pronouncement. Many people in this day and age still believe that, if the householder fails to follow the divination, illness or disaster will surely follow. Divination is complicated beyond the abilities of average mortal mentality. To have it done properly we must refer to a specialist, who has established a fine trade for himself. We take him our floor plans, which he diagnoses in more or less the capacity of a consultant. Sometimes the diviner's suggestions run contrary to the opinions of the carpenter or the architect, and if they do, the modern architect, sad as it may seem, often has to cooperate with the mystic specialist.

When it comes to selecting a day for a structure-erecting cere-mony, for a wedding, or for a funeral, divination has the last word. Three independent day-selection cycles exist, and of course, the very best thing is to satisfy the demands of all three. Since this, unfortunately, rarely ever occurs, satisfying just two is con-sidered adequate. Every four or six days comes a *taian*, or lucky day. These days are particularly propitious, and almost all struc-ture-erection ceremonies take place on them.

It is definitely not accidental that in matters of selecting a house placement or selecting a good day for certain ceremonies and activities divination should remain alive when its force in most of society has already died. It is the rule that gives spaces direc-tionality and the module that establishes temporal cycles. When we lack a way of telling us strictly what to do, divination is a method that provides a certain order. It helps us select a day that is neither too early or too late. It establishes a certain life rhythm much like the customs that instruct people to rest on Sunday and eat no meat on Friday. The *taian* days establish in all private living activities a rhythmical flow that needs no more reasonable explanation than does stopping work and going to church on Sunday.

3. *Natural Expression*

In Western words for architecture we sense a manmade some-thing that opposes nature and that flaunts mankind's strength to resist. It is to be expected that such an attitude result in buildings

59. Japanese villages, dispersed and blended completely into their natural setting, totally lack conspicuous colors, lines, or a sense of volume. (Village in the Chūbu District)

60. All of the households in this village, along the line of an ancient road, are oriented in a fixed direction in relationship to that road, though the whole is not formal or ceremonious. (Village in the Chūbu District)

66   THE FORMS

61. A village in the plains like this one spreads out in all directions without relationships to road or body of water. (A village in the Kinki District)

62. Villages laid out in block pattern are rare in Japan. The accuracy with which this village was laid out in ancient times has tended to break down. It probably required the Japanese love of natural lines several hundred years to wear down the geometry.

that give a physical sense of depth, size, and grandeur through volume. In this country, on the other hand, even when we build a tower we generally attempt to give it a moderate gentle expression, not one that challenges the very skies. Japanese buildings, while manmade, are in accord with, rather than in opposition to, nature; they are a part of, not a conqueror of, nature.

In the fixed Western architectural types represented by Renaissance style or Baroque style all elements tend to create abstract lines. Even should the thing represented be a flower or a tree, it is stylized, regulated, and completely humanized to show that the world of nature is still under the controlling thumb of Man. Throughout history, however, the Japanese house is of one style only. Periods do not exist. Still there is variety; there is enough margin for variations to suit the needs of the family and their way of life.

Not only do Japanese houses demonatrate natural expression, but so do the layouts of Japanese villages. A historical development of villages laid out geometrically is almost totally lacking in this country.

In the mountains, the houses are arranged to conform with hills and valleys. In the planes, they conform with the straight block patterns of the rice fields. Rather than reform nature's pattern, the Japanese prefer to use it skilfully. They never build ramparts around or throw up great gates at the entrances of their villages. They put their shrines deep in the shade of the forests, whereas the Europeans built their churches in commanding positions in the hearts of villages so that both architectural style and placement powerfully express the building's religious significance. Villagers look up to the tower when the bells ring. The only comparable structure in a Japanese village is the fire watchtower, a simple ladder-like affair with a bronze bell hanging in the top to sound the alarm in case of conflagration. The self-protective and totally non-religious function of the only towering building in a Japanese village is a clear indication of the national attitude toward building placement.

4. The Ancient Architectural Image

In ancient periods in all countries, vastness of scale is prevalent in architectural remains. In slave societies the world over, this vastness rose from the sacrifices of the laboring classes. Though Japan's ancient past left monuments of great size, exaggerated vastness is absent. Although the burial mound of the Emperor Nintoku is said to have consumed more actual labor than the building of the Egyptian pyramids, it has now receded into its natural setting. Religious architecture in all countries prizes a sense of eternity and a memorial quality. The most important of the Japanese shrines, the Ise Shrine, however, is rebuilt every 20 years. This would suggest that though the people wish to preserve the form, they cherish no image of a building as an eternal unchanging entity. The custom of rebuilding the shrine is said to have originated with the practice of building temporary divinity halls at yearly shrine festivals. After all, the gods were only supposed to come to earth at festival times. Why should there be dwelling places for them when they reside elsewhere? In fact, many shrines still build temporary additional stalls for festivals, and the divinity hall used in the coronation of the emperor is an entirely temporary structure that is torn down shortly after the ceremony. In all likelihood, the practice of regarding shrine buildings as temporary made it easy for the Japanese to accept without resistance the notion of rebuilding things.

63. This tomb of a fourth-century emperor is a hill covered in trees and surrounded by a double moat. (Burial mound of the Emperor Nintoku, Kinki District)

In the groves visible in all the illustrations from 59 to 62 reside the village deities. The Japanese gods frequently have some connection with the ancestors of the people, and the emperor's tomb is a grove because his divinity made this a suitable resting place.

5. *An Aesthetic that Overcomes Poverty*

Bearing up under poverty was a marked aspect of the residential restrictions imposed on the people by the government during the Edo period. Regulations, all in accordance with social level, governed everything from the way an entranceway to a house was planned to the fitting of the horizontal wooden members in the rooms. Lower ranking samurai and townspeople were forbidden to ornament *fusuma* with paintings. Similar strict controls extended even to the kind of clothes one wore.

The restrictions on houses fell into three categories; those concerning fire prevention, those concerning frugality, and those concerning formality. Since all of the buildings in those days were wooden, it is not remarkable that fifty percent of the housing regulations pertained to fire prevention and applied to all social classes. Forty percent concerned simplicity and frugality and applied to samurai, merchants, and farmers. The remaining ten percent covered questions of formality and applied to all samurai below the daimyo rank.

In addition, since Edo (Tōkyō) burned down many times and in doing so lost a great deal of property and goods, the government, as a fire-prevention step, forbade thatched roofs in the city. The compulsory use of tiles worked a financial hardship on many of the less affluent.

In the mid-Edo period, strict controls, applied even to small matters of interiors, suppressed any bold new changes of the house and fostered minute manipulations of materials. The Japanese concept of form found vent, not in dynamic images of the house, but in small ways of devising variety within the strictness of governmental controls. The people had no choice but to learn to be extremely dexterous in handling simple natural materials.

Though the Japanese house, with its carefully planed unfinished woods and its obviously clay walls may look small from the viewpoint of Occidental scale, it preserves a fine harmonious balance with nature. Even today, in the face of a modernized and dynamically industrial society, the Japanese mind undeniably regards simple natural materials as the ideal. The ability to discover harmony and beauty in simplicity is the foundation of the Japanese aesthetic.

5. THE JAPANESE ATTITUDE TOWARD SPACE

1. Spatial Concept

When I say that no Japanese word corresponds exactly to the English word "room," I am really saying that the Western concept of space does not exist for the Japanese. Although the word "*ma*" resembles "room" in meaning the Japanese thing is much too open to equate with the English concept since most of the partitions in a Japanese house are simple movable affairs. Perhaps in translating "*ma*" we would be nearer the mark to say "place." A *ma* is a space that we cannot necessarily visualize. Post placement suggests the limits of the *ma* but does not define them. Although a person has actual experience with *ma*, explaining them precisely in words is difficult. This lack of ability to give concrete expression to an idea is a great problem throughout Japanese culture. For instance, the unique and famous Japanese aesthetic of *wabi* and *sabi*, a refined and semi-rustic beauty with subtle undertones and colorations, has resulted in spatial expressions that the ordinary Japanese cannot accurately explain.

Since Japanese culture has always avoided the concrete treatment and directed its interest soley to spiritural makeup, it lacks a systemized science. For instance, Newton watched the perfectly ordinary occurrence of an apple falling from a tree. This he developed theoretically into the law of gravity. Had a Japanese seen that same apple fall, he would, without doubt, have fallen into a muse on mutability and on the impending doom awaiting all living things. The extreme emphasis on Japanese-style emotion indicates a lack of a firm theoretical structure that could have prompted a stage-by-stage development in our nation's architecture.

2. Divisions

A look at an ancient Japanese architectural plan leaves us with a clear idea of where the posts are but with a very vague notion of the walls. Dr. Masaru Sekino has reconstructed, on the basis of documents preserved in the Shōsōin of the Tōdai-ji, in Nara, the temporary palace erected in 743 for Fujiwara-no-Toyonari. This Nara period aristocrat's residence is the basis on which the Heian period later developed the *shinden*-style mansion. The Fujiwara plan is a simple rectangle with deep secondary lean-to roofed sections on the north and south. The partitioning

74

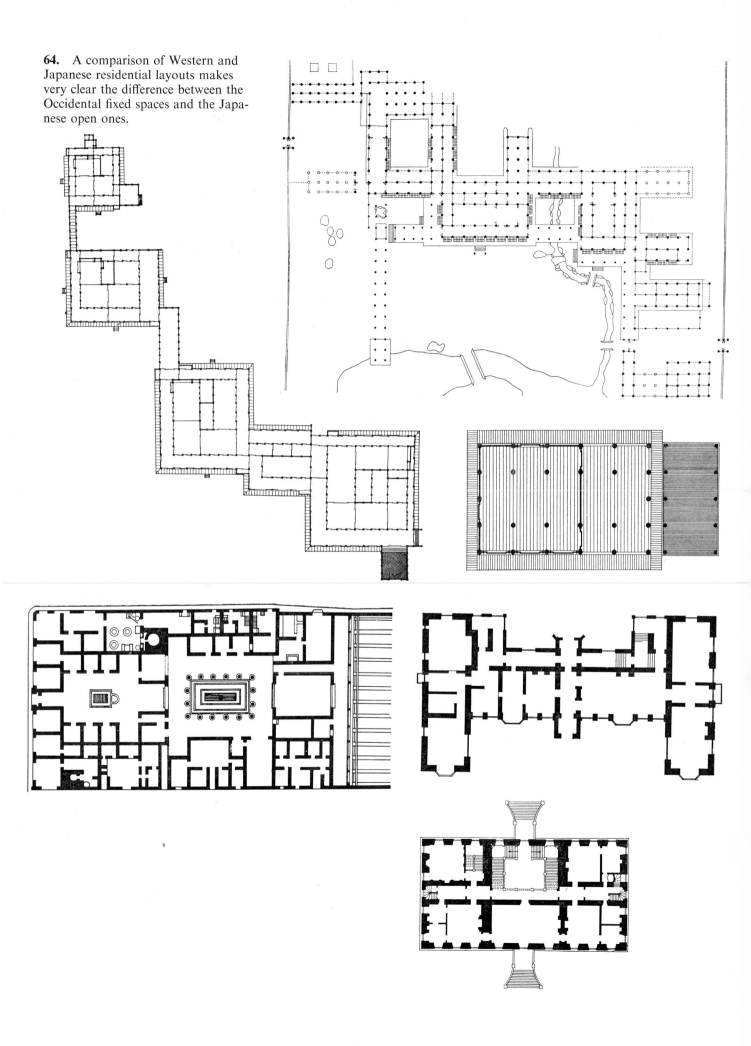

64. A comparison of Western and Japanese residential layouts makes very clear the difference between the Occidental fixed spaces and the Japanese open ones.

is indicated by straight lines from post to post. The interior is simply the inside of the rectangle divided up. Obviously the emphasis is on the posts not on the walls. If we turn to the plan of the Higashi Sanjō Palace in Kyoto, a Heian building in the *shinden* style, we seem to find ourselves confronted with something much more elaborate, but in fact, there too the plan is extremely simple. Using an imaginary fixed grid, the designers put their posts at the crosspoints of the grid lines just as they saw fit. The method is largely like the one used in the Fujiwara mansion.

When we come down to more recent times and examine the Edo-period Nijō Palace we find basically the same thing, except that certain subtle changes in daily life have gradually introduced complexities.

Since they were at liberty to divide spaces as they wanted, the Japanese developed an original method of using a three-*shaku* (One *shaku* is just under a foot.) grid. By putting two of these grids together they came up with a basic unit 6 *shaku* long and three *shaku* wide. This size is just about enough sleeping space for one person. Stood on end, it is just the right size for a door; just right that is for anyone under six feet, and most Japanese are. Since the scale is used thoroughly throughout the house, it makes house design easy, but it also makes houses monotonous. The grid plan became the basic theory of Japanese houses, however, and lasted unchanged to the present.

Western or Mid-Eastern floor plans usually use thick lines to show where the walls are and breaks in those lines to indicate the openings. The space is clearly defined or not because of the presence or absence of walls. Columns are used only for reinforcement. Since the plans do not use a grid like the Japanese one, it is impossible to imagine spaces just from the column placement.

What is the reason for this difference in approach?

3. Connections

Let us first direct our attention to structure. If our material is wood we have three structural possibilities: we can use the log-cabin (*azekura*) style found in Switzerland and Italy, we can pile our materials up to make bearing walls, or we can use the post and beam method. The log-cabin style is so much like stone building that the closed-in spaces of both are similar. Making even a few openings becomes a difficulty. Bearing walls, wooden, stone, or brick, call for first the wall structural body and then the floors and roof. Since the structure is only complete when the whole thing is complete, here again large windows or other openings can be dangerous. Most Western wooden architecture falls into one or the other of these two styles. If we want to divide our

65. Houses in Canada. Good examples of the structural style in which panel-like walls give support.

spaces with complete freedom and to be able to use large openings wherever we want, we must fall back on the post and beam structure: first erect the posts, then lay the beams on them. Though the last method is the most difficult of the wooden structural systems, it is also the best. Since walls are unnecessary, the spaces are open by their very nature. The post becomes a symbol, and we are free to use it as a hint from whch to conjure up our spaces.

Spaces in masonry buildings are, by their very natures, enclosed. When we want a window or a door, we must cut holes in the walls. Since there are limitations to the sizes of spaces possible with masonry or adobe, to build a big house, we must create many small spaces and join them. Houses I have seen in Alberobello in Italy are classic examples of this method, which does not fundamentally alter in concept in Gothic cathedrals.

A Western house is designed first, let us say, with the right number of bedrooms. The next consideration might be the dining room, then the living room, and the maid's room, all placed

77   THE JAPANESE ATTITUDE TOWARD SPACE

66. Houses in southern Switzerland. A method of piling logs one on the other similar to the Japanese *azekura* style.

67. A house in Norway, showing what the log houses of this region look like on the inside.

68. A detail of the *azekura*-like log house in Norway.

69. A Japanese house in the Chūbu District. An example of post and beam structure.

around a more or less central hall. The function of all the house's spaces is consciously set from the very beginning. The rooms' names are always carefully indicated and their functions rigidly fixed. The idea that, when all of the unit spaces needed to satisfy the needs of a family are brought together, that aggregate is a house, is the Western concept of residential architecture. The drawback is that functional alterations are not easy in this arrangement.

In the Japanese setup, from the very beginning, rooms are only imperfectly partitioned, so that later functional changes make no difference whatsoever.

The classic example of creating spaces on the basis of post placement remains today in the so-called *ta-no-ji* (shaped like the character *ta*, 田) farmhouse. The house has two rooms arranged in a line on one side of a square and two more arranged farther inward so that it actually looks like the character for the rice field in which the Japanese grow the main staple of their diet. In all likelihood, this style did not originate with farmers. Some people believe it to be a latter-day copy of the houses of the samurai. This is because the feeling of real farm life one gets from a true farmhouse, with its earthen floor and its adjacent sleeping room, is missing in the two inner rooms of the *ta-no-ji* house.

Be that as it may, the house clearly shows how the Japanese determine spatial size by partitioning on the basis of posts.

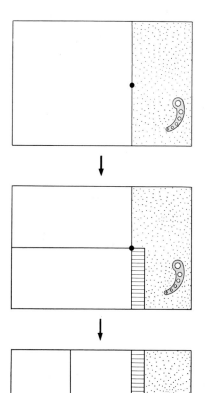

70. The evolution of the square *ta-no-ji* house. The large black dot in the middle is the *daikoku* column, and the six smaller white ones arranged in a comma shape represent the hearth. That part of the house has an earthen floor, while the other section would be floored in either boards or *tatami*. *Tatami* are not shown in the chart for the sake of clarity.

(*right*)
71. The hearth, at the boundary between the earthen-floor and *tatami* sections serves as a place to heat water and to make soups. The large column is the *daikoku* column.

6. RESIDENTIAL FORMS

1. Particularly Japanese Features

Since purely period changes in Japanese design are practically nonexistent and the only differences are ones of locale, we might say the concept of inclusive styles has failed to develop here. For this reason, in talking of Japanese houses, we are safer to deal with forms instead of styles.

Modern Japanese husbands and wives consider the "home" their own dwelling place, the special unit that they are to inhabit with their children, but in the history of the Japanese house, this simple structure is the exception rather than the rule. In ancient times, the home included, as well as places for sleeping and cooking, the spot where food was grown, and in the middle-ages it also came to include an area for the production of commercial products as well as a place for negotiations about those products. Even the homes of royalty and of the aristocracy would be unthinkable without office-like spaces devoted to ceremonial functions. Farmhouses in northeast Honshū and in certain other areas of Japan often include both space for farm work and stable space for horses and cows.

a. Farmhouses
Even today, the most frequent farmhouse type is the *ta-no-ji*, in which the rooms all lack fixed functions. The significance of the *fusuma* that divides the main space into four sections is vague. They do not actually cut one space off from another. At certain times, two of the rooms can serve as one, and at others, all four of them can become one big room. Here again we see a case in which the English word "room" is not really applicable. What the *fusuma* create is four *ma*, or sections, not four rooms in the strict sense. Although the opening and closing of the *fusuma* make possible a rich variety of spatial combinations, none of the *ma* so created provides anything near complete privacy. In the earthen-floor section of the house the residents can continue their chores even in cold or snowy weather, and even the cows and horses find a corner to warm themselves.

b. Pointed-roof Houses
The combination work area and residence of huge pointed-roof houses in Hida, in Gifu Prefecture, the Chūbu District, is a well known relic from the days of vast families. Some of the bigger houses are as much as 30 feet tall at the ridge. The triangular

82

gable end is as steep as would be the sides of a book slightly open and stood on its sides. The reed thatch roof is sometimes two feet thick. The entrance is on the long side of the house. No nails are used. All of the parts are either fitted with wooden pegs or tied tightly together with straw rope. The interiors are divided into four or five levels. The top two are usually lofts for raising silk worms. The noted German architect Bruno Taut praised these structures as both theoretically sound and logical.

c. Kyōto Town House

The crowded conditions of towns like Kyōto, where it was necessary to build houses up against each other, have had a great influence on the residential form, as we can see in the famous Kyōto town houses. The earth or paved space running from the street to the rear of the house and called the "garden" corresponds to the earthen-floor section of a farmhouse. Since here merchants made and sold their wares, the space is actually quite close in nature to a room. Although residents of such houses wanted as good air circulation from the front as possible they also wanted to keep out the prying eyes of passersby. The answer to the problem was lattices for the windows. Lattices allow a passage of air, but keep out uninvited callers. The Japanese have never used the sort of horizontal louvers one sees frequently in the West, because deep eaves in Japanese houses eliminate the need for a sun shade and because horizontal louvers collect dust.

d. Houses in Kurashiki

In the city of Kurashiki, which thrived during the Edo period, we find houses of a type suggesting Western architecture. Though the structures are wooden, the houses themselves are entirely covered with plaster. Sliding doors are used, but they are more like doors and windows in the West than like the traditional Japanese *fusuma* and *shōji*. The fact is that most of the houses were less houses than storehouses, though quite a number of them did actually provide places of residence.

2. *From Space to Function*

In the history of the house in this country, the one form that most closely resembles urban houses of today is the residence of medieval samurai. We can trace the lineage of this form back still further to the aristocrats' homes of earlier times. The secret behind the resemblance among the three forms is that, call them samurai or call them courtiers, these men of old lived much as do today's white-collar workers in that they performed no productive activities at home. The oldest in this line of residential forms is the *shinden* style used in the mansions of noblemen of many ages past.

In the *shinden* houses, the usual dwelling of the general aristoc-

72. The third and fourth floors of farmhouses in mountainous regions serve as lofts for breeding silkworms. (A so-called *gasshō* (praying-hands) pointed roof farmhouse in Shirakawa Village, the Chūbu District)

73. Most often the interiors of such farmhouses are floored with boards.

74. A group of *gasshō* style houses hidden in a valley.

86   THE FORMS

75. Though located in mountainous regions, just like that of the *gasshō*-houses, other houses without particular cottage industries, such as silk worm breeding, lose their distinctive traits. The stones on the roof are to keep the cypress shingles from blowing away in the wind.

76. A farmhouse in the Chūgoku District. (Kurashiki)
White plaster walls and a classic tile roof characterize the building. The first-story windows are fitted with a kind of slender lattice used throughout western Japan.

Kurashiki

77. Note the tile reinforcement insets in the walls of these houses in the city of Kurashiki.

78. Floor plan of a merchant's house in the same region.
The figures indicate the number of *tatami* mats used in that room.
A–godown, B–entrance hall, C–kitchen, D–storage, E–inner garden, F–shop, G–veranda, H–bath, I–toilet.

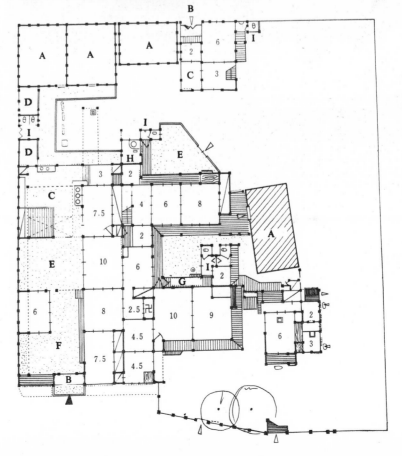

Osaka

79. Farmhouse in the Kinki District (Osaka).
The posts and beams, visible on the outside, contrast beautifully with the white of the plaster walls. This is the seventeenth-century Yoshimura House.

80. Interior of the Yoshimura house. The irregular sizes of posts and beams are a distinctive feature of houses of the Kinki area.

81. Floor plan of the Yoshimura house.

82. Ceiling plan of the Yoshimura house.

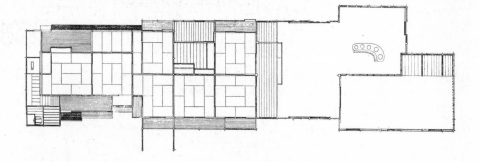

88 THE FORMS

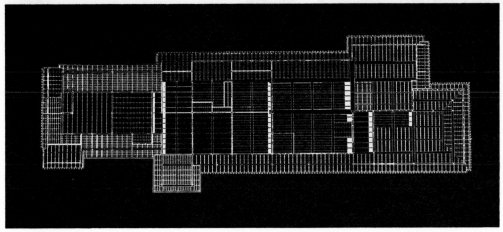

89 RESIDENTIAL FORMS

83. A house in the Kanto region. The upper storage story features thick plaster walls and heavy window shutters to protect against fire. A wealthy merchant built this house and displayed his wealth in the massive demon-plate finials on the ends of the ridge. So abundant, indeed, is the sense of affluence that the traditional Japanese simplicity has fallen by the wayside.

84. A godown window from the Kanto District.

91 RESIDENTIAL FORMS

85. Floor plan of a Kinki District merchant's house. A–earthen floored area, B–shop, C–entrance, D–kitchen, E–inner room, F–inner garden, G–toilet and bath.

86. A house in the Kinki District. Notice the very fine lattice work in the windows of both the upper and the lower stories. (Kyoto)

87. Inclined palings in front of a Kinki District house.

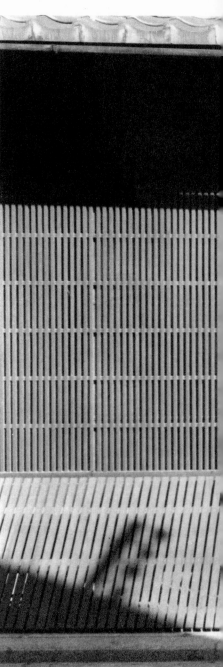

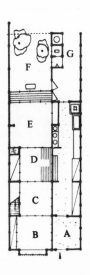

93 RESIDENTIAL FORMS

racy of the Heian period, there existed a certain ideal image. That image included the main section of the house, the *seiden*, which stood almost in the exact center of the site and faced south. To the east, west, and north, or to the northwest and northeast of the *seiden* stood other smaller buildings. Each of the buildings was independent, but all were connected by means of covered walkways. The master of the house resided in the *seiden* and his family in the outer buildings. Beyond these stood a miscellaneous collection of other buildings for retainers and servants. In the early days of this form, all of the buildings maintained a strict right-left symmetry, but gradually the house became less strictly arranged, lost its symmetry, and became more practically planned. As the ruling power gradually switched from the hands of the court nobles to those of the warrior class, so, the prevailing residential form changed from the *shinden* to the *shoin* style. Not only is the plan of the *shoin* house freer than that of the *shinden*, but it marks a development of certain types of equipment functionally better suited to the warrior's way of living.

Although we cannot divide Japanese residential architectural history into clear styles the way we can that of the West, we do notice a distinction between houses before the Kamakura (1185–1333) and Muromachi periods (1338–1573), when the *shinden* prevailed, and later, when the *shoin* held sway. With the passing of the influence of court nobles, their elegant formal houses tended to die out, and with the ascent of the warrior class, residential buildings tended more to simplicity and strength. Though we see the influence of the *shinden* in the *shoin* arrangement of main hall in front and private dwelling quarters behind, the *shoin* main building is functionally much more advanced than in the older style.

3. *Differences between the* Shinden *and the* Shoin

Shinden buildings were made of unfinished wood and were roofed with cypress-bark shingles. All of the floors were boarded. The interior contained very few partitions, and hanging bamboo blinds, called *sudare*, were the main method of separating one area from another. Much in the style of stage sets, simple furniture, usually only round straw mats for sitting, elbow rests, on occasion a low table or a simple folding chair, came and went as the moment demanded.

The main hall of a *shoin* house, however, very much resembles the *ta-no-ji* form of the commoners' houses, except that the innermost section, the *jōdan-no-ma*, was raised a step from the main floor level. Toward the end of the Muromachi period, the warrior's house gained an entrance room (*genkan*) and a completed *zashiki*, or main sitting room, with a *tokonoma*, ornamental shelves, and *shoin* window, a sort of bay window with a shelf-desk for writing. The *shoin* room is said to have originated as a study room in the homes of Buddhist priests. It is likely that with the advent of the aesthetically minded Ashikaga shoguns of the Muromachi period, the styles of living of court nobles, priests, and warriors began to influence each other so that not just the cleric but the man of arms also felt a need for a room in which to study and to receive guests. The *shoin* room and the many changes rung on it have become the basic feature of the Japanese house, even as it exists today. The *tokonoma* itself is said to have evolved from the abbreviated Buddhist altars found in priests' homes. At first, a Buddhist painting was hung on the wall and a board shelf arranged below it to hold various ritual articles. Later the arrangement became a built-in and permanent part of the room. Earlier, *tatami* had been used only in certain areas of the house, but with the perfection of the *shoin* style, it became the general practice to use them throughout the house. Shingle roofs declined in favor of the classic tile roofing in this age.

In the *shinden* house, floor coverings and furniture were brought into incomplete spaces to serve the purpose of the moment in a system that prized form above function. The functional divisions made possible by the opening and closing of the *fusuma* in the *shoin* house, however, represent the culmination of the Japanese house's distinctive fusion of space and time. I mean by this a space that is capable of conforming to temporal and functional changes.

From the Momoyama (1568–1615) to the Edo periods (1615–1867), the form of the commoner's house crystalized. In the Edo period, too, the use of an entrance room, and a sitting room with a *tokonoma*, ornamental shelves, and a *shoin* formalized and extended from the general commoner's house, itself a social phenomenon of the age, even to the farmhouse.

4. The Tea House

Up till this point, we have been discussing the main currents in the development of the Japanese house, but we must not omit the important, though independent, tea house because it has exerted a great influence on other residential buildings.

Tea was not imported into this country from China until the middle-ages. From the Kamakura into the Muromachi periods, people of upper society often offered tea to guests, and they soon found that a shelf for holding the tea-making equipment was essential. At first this shelf was an ordinary affair kept in the room (the *tsugi-no-ma*) next to the main room, but it later developed into something more elaborate and came to serve as an important ornament in the main room itself. The upper classes are said to have indulged in a game in those days in which teas of different qualities and kinds were passed among guests who had to identify

88. Interior of a tea house. The bent column next to the small hearth is of great significance.

them by their flavors. Priests of the same era who studied Zen Buddhism, another import from China, often offered their guests tea to drink but in a style far simpler than the aristocrats' sophisticated pastime.

The famous tea master Sen-no-Rikyū gave completed form to the tea ceremony in an extremely simple and sincere version. Rikyū's ceremony is a reaction against the elaborate tea drinking parties and the general artistic trends of his day. According to him, to properly taste the tea and to increase the feeling of relaxation the tea should bring, the proper environment for the ceremony is of great importance.

Later it became the recognized custom to close oneself in a small room (4 1/2 mats) to drink tea because in that small place one created his own universe of calm and peace away from the noise of the world. Tea masters thus gave birth to the art of ridding oneself of tensions and entering a free world of contemplation. The influence of this attitude resulted in tea houses that avoid formalism, that are above all extremely simple and asymmetrical. Sizes gradually dwindled from the earlier 4 1/2 mats to 3, then to 2 3/4 and finally to 1 3/4. The smaller the better, as long as movements could be made small enough to promote psychological concentration.

Tea-house architecture, a negative reaction to its age, disavowed formality more than anything else and sought to manifest primarily the simplicity of rural and mountain moods. Its ultra-refined content, however, made the tea house an urban and a cultural thing. Freedom is the most revered aspect of the tea ceremony, and the beauty of forms with something missing, or the abbreviated forms, is one of its most important points.

Even though a tea house might be square in plan, the designer always felt it necessary to break the symmetry somehow through his use of *tokonoma*, windows, or ceiling. On the other hand, in the effort to create asymmetry he ran the danger of producing a mood of instability or restlessness, and he had to pay great attention to the proper balance of lines and surfaces. The desire for balance led to an extreme fondness for natural, simple, unprocessed materials, wood with the bark still on, bamboo, grasses, and clay in their natural shapes and colors. The ideal of the tea house is the calm and quiet of materials in their natural state. The intermediate colors, even the dark colors, of nature combined with the pure white paper of the *shōji*, themselves placed lower than the normal line of sight or divided up into many smaller panels, created in the small space of the room an unusually rich lighting effect. The wistful, somber, and subtle refinement of *wabi* and *sabi*, the essential elements in Japanese aesthetics, finds its most direct expression in the tea house. Many people had their own tea houses with this sort of calm composed atmosphere, where finding repose from the noise of the world rapidly became a favorite indulgence.

96 THE FORMS

98   THE FORMS

89. Another tea-house interior.

90. Tea-house floor plans. The dotted lines indicate the *tatami* mats.

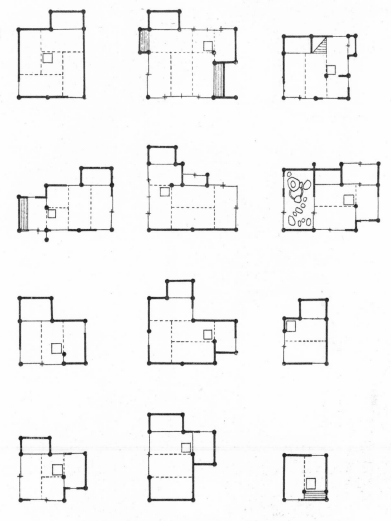

5. The Tea-House Setting

The proper tea ceremony, as practised widely in the middle-ages, begins in the garden. The invited guests move over garden stepping stones set in a deep carpet of moss along the one of a number of routes that the host has chosen for the day and has indicated by using *ishimusubi*, stones bound in rope and set on stepping stones where the guests are *not* to go. Following the chosen path, the guests progress, enjoying the view, till they arrive at a small rustic waiting house. Such waiting stations are usually no more than a simple roof with a plain bench on which to sit and wait. Often the gurgling of flowing water delights the ear in these places, where it is a joy to rest awhile. As the guest continues along the path he will soon see a stone washing basin into which a flume constantly pours a stream of crystal water. Using the gracefully proportioned bamboo dipper, always provided, the guest will wash his hands in water from the basin and rinse out his mouth. A few steps from the basin is the tea house. The entrance to the building is a narrow, low affair only two feet or so high. To get in, one sits on the door frame, removes his

99 RESIDENTIAL FORMS

101 RESIDENTIAL FORMS

(*preceding pages*)
91. *Ishimusubi*, a stone, about the size of a clenched fist, tied with rope, indicates that one should not pass. It is usually placed on top of stepping stones or a path.

92. A tea house and garden at the Katsura Detached Palace.
This is a very large building as teahouses, usually very small, go.

sandals (*zōri*), raises both legs to the floor of the room, changes his direction, and finds himself seated in the tiny tea room. The guest merely greets the host and takes his own place. Though physically the room may be small (usually 4 1/2 and sometimes as small as 2 mats) it is spiritually spacious. Gradually one's spirit calms. In the tea room, it does not do to discuss politics, work, or other topics pertaining to human glory or vanity. One should discard station and rank when he enters the door. Each man present is free, and this freedom extends to the architecture itself, where it is possible to alter *tatami* sizes and to ignore rules and styles. The hot water for the tea is ready in a special boiler on a small hearth. The master of the ceremony, following strictly prescribed procedures, places a small quantity of powdered green tea in a treasured tea bowl, adds water, and beats the tea with a bamboo whisk till it is frothy. He then offers it to his guests.

Accentuating the mood of simplicity and sincerity are the smaller-than usual *tokonoma* with its rough clay walls, the unfinished columns with the bark remaining on them, and the woven bamboo ceiling.

part three
THE SYSTEMS

7. SPACE

NOT ONLY THE CLIMATE AND TOPOGRAPHY of the land but the physical bodies and actions of the Japanese people themselves influenced the shaping of the Japanese house. Harmony with the body must be maintained in the house. For an idea of how this fits the Japanese residence we must turn our attention briefly to physiology. Dr. Tadashi Misawa, M.D., claims that Japanese people from the upper social strata are closer in body configuration to Westerners of similar social strata than are those of lower levels. A second physiologist holds that leg lengths vary considerably between the children of Japanese families who use both chairs and the traditional Japanese method of sitting on the *tatami* covered floor and those who never use chairs.

From these two facts we can suppose that the physiology of the Japanese is not merely a matter of racial characteristics but that it also bears the clear stamp of long years of repeated dietary and living habits. Dr. Misawa suggests that if all Japanese people were of the upper classes and ate the same kind of food, they could possibly approach physiques similar to those of Occidental peoples. The second physiologist's evidence indicates that the shortness of the Japanese leg is the result of many ages of sitting in a particular way. Since the Japanese leg is short, the body's center of gravity is lower. This perhaps has some connection with the ancient fondness for working in a crouching or semi-standing position. Whether the squatting is a result of the lower center of gravity or the center of gravity's position is where it is because of the habit of squatting I cannot say, but the fact remains that the Japanese consider this a restful posture. Many areas in the Japanese house, such as the bath and the toilet, require one to assume the squat.

Some say that our customs of taking small steps, not swinging the arms too wide, and trying not to raise the feet too high while walking derive from the inconvenience a wide gait would cause someone clad in kimono and from the danger of stirring up the dust on he t*tatami*. At any rate, obviously the Japanese house is intimately connected both with the Japanese way of living and with the physiology of the Japanese body.

105

1. The Open-plan House

When I say that the Japanese house uses an open plan, I mean that the windows and doors are big and open wide. To amplify, I do not consider the modern architectural use of large permanently fixed glass areas open plan. Although these windows are open in the sense that what is on the other side is visible, they are definitely closed in that they do not allow the passage of sound, air, people or anything else but light.

It would be as unreasonable to use an open-plan house in a noisy dusty area as it would be to build a tightly closed house in a wonderful natural setting. The environment, that is whether there is plenty of light and fresh air and whether the views from the windows are good, determines the quality of the house.

The openness of the Japanese house is actually an openness within an enclosed area in that a fence cuts it off from the outside world. Of course, if the windows and doors were less wide no fence at all, or at most a simple one, would be perfectly adequate. Inside the fence is a garden separated from the interior of the house by sliding rain shutters (*amado*) and glass doors, or in times past by paper covered *shōji*. These outer sliding doors vary very little from the *shōji* and *fusuma* used as interior space dividers.

Fusuma and *shōji*, though partitions are not perfect ones, and sounds and the presence of someone in the next room are easily detectable through them. They effectively provide a visual block, but since they do not cut off sounds, it is bad to put a room whose activities are boisterous next to one in which quiet is important.

In contrast with the openness of Japanese houses, Western houses with individual rooms shut off by thick walls and doors and windows are more clearly parceled off. The house, in general, is like a number of neighboring cells. In a structure like this, all one needs to do is shut the door, and sounds from other rooms

An example of using a single room for many purposes in winter.

93. Breakfast.

94. Daytime amusements.

95. Evening family get-together.

96. Sleeping.

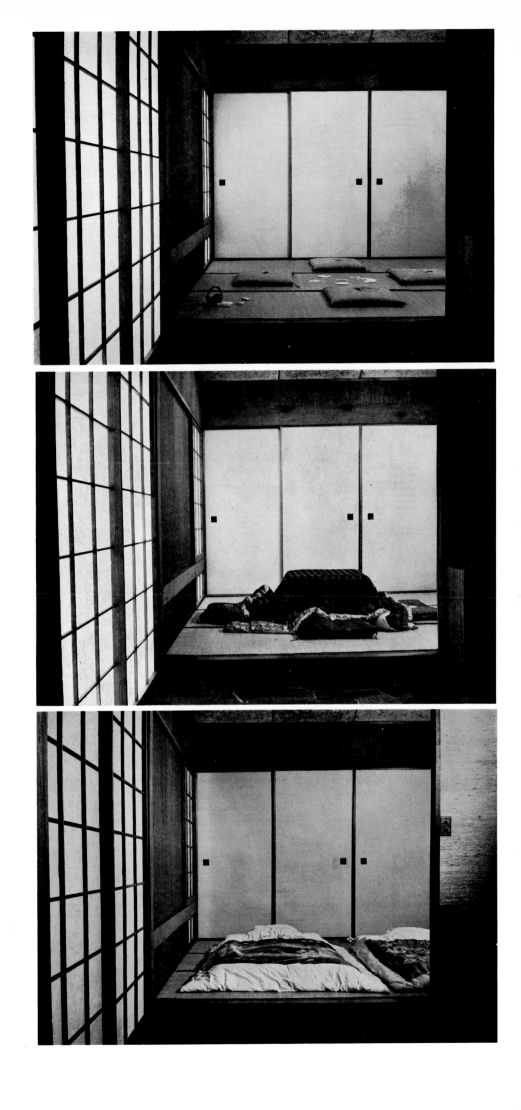

become inaudible. The one room is completely isolated from all others. In this arrangement fences around houses are frequently superfluous.

2. All-purpose Spaces

The West operates on the idea that each function has its own space. Eating requires suitable space, as does sleeping. The very names bedroom, dining room, bathroom, clearly show the attitude that one function should have one designated room shut off from the other spaces by four walls. The Japanese house, however, names its rooms by their location—*okuzashiki*, the inner sitting room or *nakanoma*, the middle room—without direct reference to function. In other words, from the outset the Westerner thinks in terms of function and makes his rooms accordingly, whereas the Japanese simply sets up zones. Rather than letting the function create the room, he isolates the room from the function. For instance, practically every house has one, or maybe two, rooms called *zashiki*. We have said that the word means sitting room, when, in fact, it means little more than "room," though in most instances it is the room farthest in from the street and usually the most elegantly appointed. It is the place in which to receive guests or the room where the master of the house does his reading or studying. If a guest decides to stop the night, he will sleep in the *zashiki*, and it is most certainly in the *zashiki* that he would receive his meals. The space called *zashiki* is simply the most ceremonious of the house's rooms, but it has no one specific function. The same thing is true of the so-called *cha-no-ma*. Ordinarily this is the room where the family takes its meals, but in many families, when night somes, someone will sleep in the *cha-no-ma*.

97. Comparisons between the functional approaches to spaces in the West and in Japan.

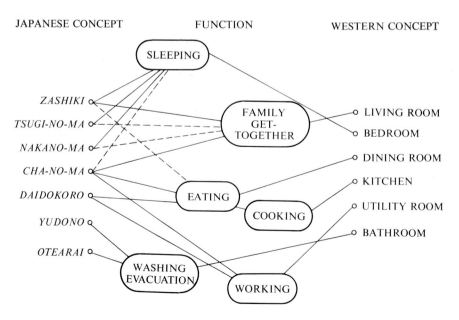

Ways of altering spatial expanse by opening and closing *fusuma*.

98. All closed.

99. Open on one side.

100. Open on two sides.

101. Open on three sides.

3. Connecting Spaces

Japanese spaces, instead of having a fixed function, suit the function to the occasion and need. In other words, the use to which a space is put varies with the time of day. The size of a given space freely changes as we open or close the *fusuma*.

The notion of continuous and interrupted spatial flow pervades even the storage spaces, the *oshi-ire,* which are treated much as the actual living spaces. Although now these "closets" are divided halfway up to make a shelf for bedding, in earlier times they were not designed to contain any particular kind of thing. The same grid used in the living spaces is also used in laying out the storage spaces, and the *fusuma* used for them are exactly like those used everywhere else in the house. This means that the closet spaces are considered continuous with the living spaces. Although the width of the closet opening is most commonly six feet, it could be nine feet or twelve feet, but the depth is always three feet. From the outside, however, they are so much a part of the general spatial atmosphere that even a Japanese person cannot always say for sure by just looking whether *fusuma* leads to a closet, the next room, or a corridor.

The identical nature of closet *fusuma* and regular partitioning *fusuma* gives the Japanese residential space an air of boundless secrecy. Surrounded by entrances to neighboring rooms, to corridors, or to closets, one is prompted to imagine what lies beyond. When he is positive that the *fusuma* conceal a closet, he may open them to find another room. This sense of dramatically unfolding space is essential to the Japanese house.

8. FUNCTION

1. A Functional House

Mainly in terms of space, Japanese interiors are flexible and conform readily to the needs of the people living in them. Speaking from the viewpoint of function, on the other hand, since these interiors conform to a number of needs, they actually serve no fixed function at all. The fact is that because a traditional Japanese room has no furniture inherent to it, when a person from another country, to whom a furnitureless room is unliveable, glances at a photograph of a bare Japanese room in a magazine he naturally assumes that no one lives in the house portrayed. A room without furniture is a functional void. In the West, a bedroom serves as a bedroom because it has a bed in it and because you can close its doors. Similarly, a dining room is a dining room because it has cupboards, table, and chairs and because it is near enough to the kitchen to make carrying food back and forth easy. In other words, the equipment in these rooms is ready from the beginning, whereas in a Japanese room it is not. When a bed is needed, the Japanese bring it in, and when a table is required, they bring that in too. In other words, the Japanese house is functionally flexible.

2. The Effect of Movable Furniture

Most ordinary Japanese "dining rooms" consist of a low simple movable, or even folding, table in the middle of the room with cushions for sitting (*zabuton*) spread around it on the floor. Should a guest come, no table, but only the cushions are adequate appointment to make the same room a reception room. In such cases the tea and cakes offered as refreshment might be left on the tray on which they were brought in or they might be put directly on the *tatami*. If the lady of the house needs to iron something or has some sewing to do she merely brings in the equipment she needs and does it all in the same room. When the family gets together after dinner for chatting or some sort of games, all they need do to make the space suitable is rearrange the cushions a little. When bedtime comes, just pull the bedding out of the closet, put it right on the *tatami*, and we have a bedroom. Many families use small low electric lamps designed for use by the pillow side at night.

Still more interesting, when a crowd of people gets together,

102. A functionally flexible interior.

the *fusuma* can be easily removed to make of the interior spaces something very like a stage, with the garden representing the darkened auditorium. Since people sit on the floor, no need to make arrangements for a chair for each individual. Even a small house can accommodate a fairly large number of guests. I should mention, however, that with the rise in economic conditions, and the spread of Western-style living, more and more families are abandoning the multi-purpose room system in favor of a partial unit-functional system.

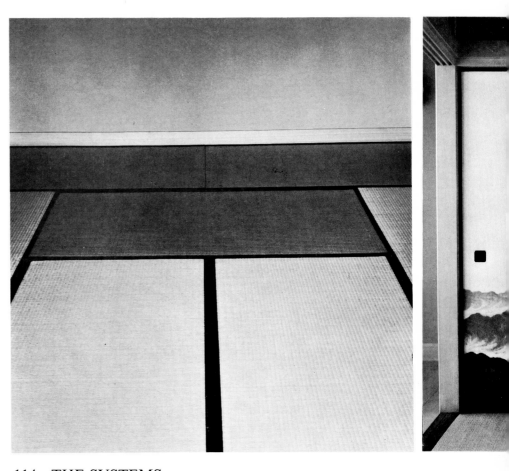

9. DIMENSION

1. The Japanese Scale of Measurement

Although the culture of the town, that flourished in the Edo period, was significant in many fields, we must not overlook the great contribution it made to standardized production. It was during the Edo period that one *ken* became the standard horizontal measurement for all such things as *tatami* floor mats, *shōji*, and *fusuma*, and that the vertical measurement also became uniform. Although the measurement of the *ken* (in Tōkyō close to six feet) varies slightly from district to district, this in no way impairs the great importance of the common use of the term. After all, rigidly exact measurements are inessential to the daily acts of sleeping and coming in and going out.

The square of one *ken*, or one *tsubo*, used in measuring land area or the sizes of houses, is equivalent to the area of two *tatami* mats. The widths of posts, lintels, and door sills is 1/20 of one *ken*, and corridors are 1/2 of one *ken*, or roughly three feet,

103. A single *tatami*, three by six feet.

104. A single *fusuma* panel is the same size.

105. A single *shōji* panel is the same size.

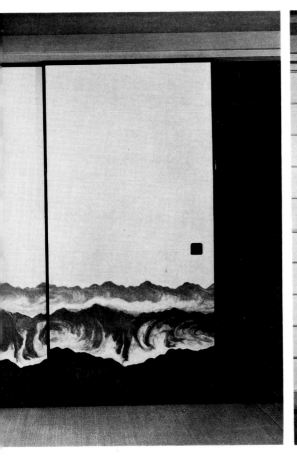

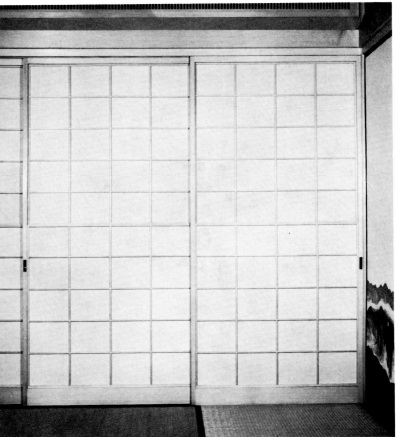

wide, the width of one *tatami* mat. As long as we adhere to this module, drawing and reading Japanese residential floor plans requires no special technical training. A man who wants to build a house, has only to tell the carpenter what he wants, discuss the matter with him, and he will have an idea of what the finished house will look like. In other words, anyone with a little interest, can make his own plans and improvizations on them just as an architect would. As long as the *tatami* size is the basis, whatever personal treatments might be used, the design will not suffer a radical loss of balance.

Although the standard *tatami* size is roughly three by six feet, auxiliary mats of three by three feet are often used. The ordinary room sizes are three mats, four and one half mats, six mats or eight mats. Other sizes are rare enough to be always exceptional. Something like a seven and one-half-mat room seems fragmentary to the Japanese mind and is particularly repugnant. As we have said, the standard closet is three by six feet, or the size of one *tatami* mat. The toilet and the washroom each occupy one half a mat. Of course, it is the physiology of the Japanese body that makes possible a satisfactory toilet in a space only three by three. Because of the length of the average Japanese arm, this space is large enough to permit a person to open and shut the hinged door—practically the only hinged door used in the Japanese house—without bumping his elbow. Lately, however, the young Japanese are getting bigger, and it has become necessary to divide a nine-foot length in half to make a toilet area three by four and one half feet. Though the floor of the bath is covered in concrete or tile, it is usually the size of two or three *tatami* mats. The shoe box in the entrance hall is generally one, two, or three *tatami* mats in area. I am not arbitrarily using the words two-*tatami* mats in size. Describing rooms by the number of mats in their area is such common usage in Japan that to avoid it is to run the risk of being unable to communicate properly. The term *jō* or one mat is used, and even when a room has a wooden floor or is carpeted, it will be described as equivalent to a three-*jō* or six-*jō* room.

From ancient times, the standardization of measurements has extended beyond architecture to include kimono, bedding, and many other aspects of Japanese life. As the product of the Japanese sense of beauty, it has a value much like that of the golden mean in the West.

2. *The Order of Measurements in Daily-living Spaces*

The paper covering on *fusuma* is a single sheet the same size as one *tatami* mat, whereas the paper for *shōji* comes on a role about ten inches wide. Whatever the variation in the shape and size of the *shōji* lattice—and they are numberless—the same paper

106. A roll of *shōji* paper.

can be used to cover them.

Cloth for kimono or for the covering of bedding mats (*futon*) come in pieces called *tan*, which are approximately fourteen inches wide and forty-two feet long, that is they are one fifth as wide as one *ken* and seven times as long. This size is calculated to be enough cloth to make a single adult kimono or to cover one bedding mat. A double length or two *tan*, called one *hiki*, is enough cloth to make covers for two bed mats, the number used by one person. The length of the usual kimono made with this cloth is left longer than needed so that when it is worn it can be folded up at about the waist to suit the height of the individual wearing it, much like the ancient Roman toga. This means that generally all kimonos are the same length and anyone can wear any kimono without resewing it by simply folding it under the right amount at the waist. Type of cloth and pattern more than shape of the kimono indicate the age of the wearer and the formality or informality of the garment. As a rule, there is only one method of making all kimono. This results in a surprisingly uniform systematization of everything from production standards to technical and design variation and to styles dictated by use of the garment or age of the wearer. By simply looking at a bolt of the cloth one can tell whether it is suited to an informal or a formal kimono. The color and pattern tell us the sex and age of the person who will wear it. This attitude toward cloth extends to the fabric used in covering the cushions on which we sit. Here again color and pattern determine the degree of formality of the completed article.

In architecture, this same sense of standardization reflects in the centuries-old *kiwari* set of rules for fixing the measurements not only of the *tatami* and *fusuma*, but of the posts, beams, rafters, and practically everything else. The *kiwari* method flourished most widely in the Momoyama period (1568-1603), but limited largely to temple buildings and the homes of the upper crust, it was too difficult and too costly ever to extend to the homes of the commonality. In the *kiwari* method, once the size of the post is set, with only a little freedom left over, the sizes of everything else are automatically fixed. Since the aim of the system was beauty of proportion, which it attempted to make into a technique, it was naturally best suited to religious buildings and the mansions of the aristocracy where proportion was particularly important.

3. *The Measurement Tradition and Modern Architecture*

We are not sure when the traditional system of measurements came to be firmly established, but we do know that it closely resembles today's wide-spread grid planning or modular planning, in which fixed floor-plan measurements are used over and over again. The modular systems are in keeping with modern society because they make use of the standardized parts and materials that result from mass production. With such standardized parts, it is essential to repeat the same forms often.

Although the Katsura Detached Palace is 300 years old, it looks very modern, largely, I believe, because its measurement system is close to today's modular planning. Plan and section are based on the length of a single *tatami* mat, and the same proportions occur again and again. All of the *shōji* and rain shutters are open to the floor and have simple horizontal and vertical lines that would conform well with mass-production standardization. Since all the horizontal and vertical lines harmonize, the building's almost unornamented design uses no mediocre additional lines or curves to achieve unwanted effects.

10. TECHNIQUES

1. Structures that Shake but Do Not Break

Although the steep Japanese house roof towers like a mountain peak, the walls underneath and the strut structure almost completely lack diagonal members. Anybody who thought about it would immediately see that diagonal bracing tightens up a structure so that it will not fall. The Japanese, too, have not missed the point as we can judge from the number of diagonal braces they use, throughout the building process. Once the house is completed, however, out come the diagonal braces. In about the sixth century, when architectural techniques from China came into this country, a number of small wooden members were used piled up over the binders between posts and beams to give strength against wind and earthquake. The system, much too bulky for use in residential buildings, found application only in large temples and pagodas. The system houses use is a flexible structure in which the building shakes with exterior forces but does not collapse.

Most Western architecture is of a rigid-structure type in which braces provide reinforcement. Japanese buildings, however, operating on the principle that it is better to bend with the wind than break, use a structure that moves with the forces and, therefore, does not fall down. The selection of such a pliant structure clearly points up the Japanese attitude toward nature.

To make a pliant structure effective, the joinery between posts and beams and foundations must be exact, or in any tremor at all the house will drop to pieces. Perhaps this is why Japanese joint details are so beautiful, or perhaps, indeed, it is the skill of Japanese hands that made the development of outstanding joinery possible. I cannot say which is the basic cause. The climate's humidity may have played an important role by rusting and reducing the life of metal reinforcements. Though in ancient buildings we find metal used in parts of doors and in door-pulls they are generally rusted to a state of crumbling. Perhaps through bitter experience the Japanese gave up on using metal parts.

Accurate joint details are the basis of the erection system in which all securing is done with wooden wedges and pegs. Japanese carpenters despise nails because to have to use them brands their techniques as inferior. Rather than structural techniques, founded on dynamics rationality, in Japan joinery techniques saw the greatest progress.

Combining both structural joints and ornamental elements,

107. Roof structure. Wooden members joined together without the help of nails, adhesives, or diagonal elements.

120 THE SYSTEMS

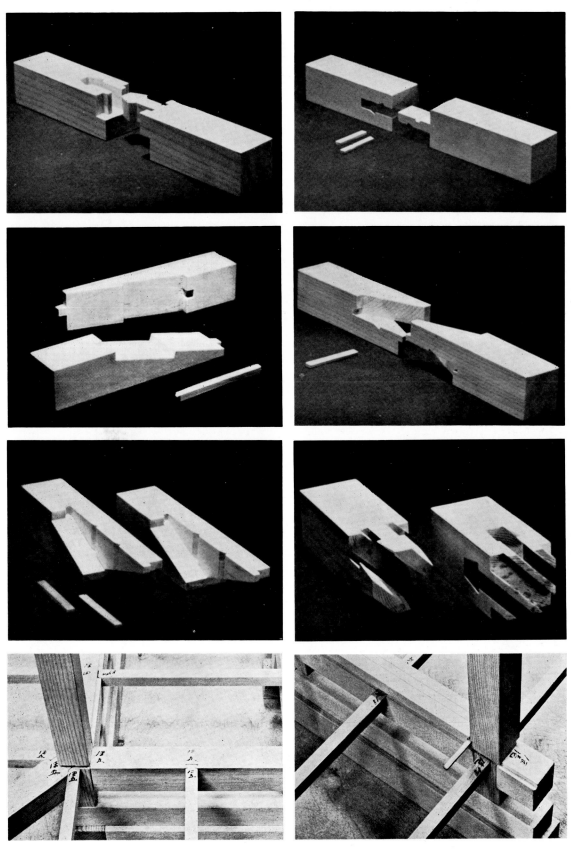

108.   A number of types of beam and post joints. (The Uchida Laboratory, Tōkyō University)

109.   The joints actually put together. (The Uchida Laboratory, Tōkyō University).

121   TECHNIQUES

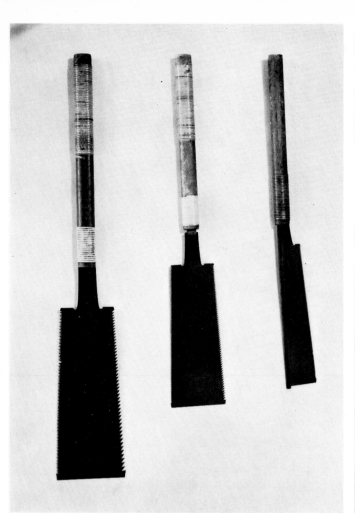

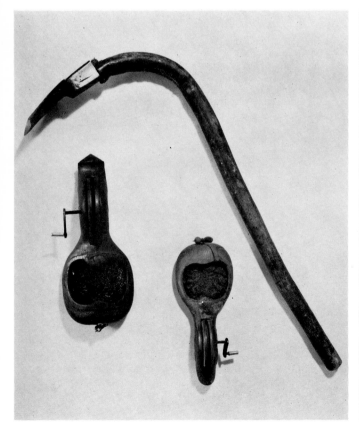

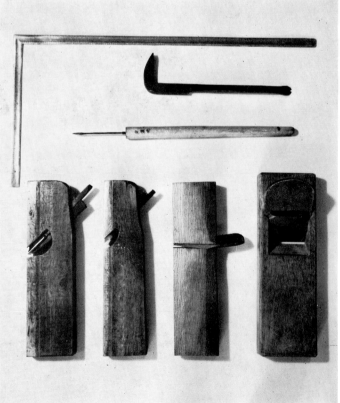

Carpenters' tools

110. Saws.

111. Hammers and chisels.

112. Carpenter's ink and string reel for making lines. Adze.

113. Top to bottom: angle rule, crowbar, gimlet, four kinds of planes.

Japanese joinery types number over 70, though only about 30 are in general use. They all fall in general classifications for lengthening, making right-angle joints, or preventing twisting distortions, but each type has a special name.

Whatever the method, two things always hold true: no nails whatsoever, and no glues or binding agents because it must be possible to erect, dismantle, and re-erect the building as many times as is necessary. Yet another important feature applicable to all carpentry, with the exception of foundations and places that naturally are never seen, is that the finished product not reveal the inner details by which the effect is achieved.

2. Joints without Nails

Meticulous joinery, demanded by the Japanese architectural structural method, is so attractive to look at that no other ornamentation is needed. In Western buildings, up till recent times, ceiling moldings and framework around doors and windows always covered up the roughness of the actual building. This never happened in Japan.

All the Japanese carpenter uses to make joints so perfect that you could not slide a needle in them is his hammer, his saw, and his chisel. Although the tools look very much like their Occidental counterparts, the way one uses them is slightly different, and I think the secret of the superiority of Japanese joinery lies in that very difference.

For instance, the teeth of a Japanese saw are set in the opposite direction from those of Western saws. This means that you cut on the upstroke rathe thanr on the downstroke. The difference is more than just direction, because in theory you can do better work cutting on the upstroke. For downstroke cutting the saw itself must be a little thicker to prevent its bending. Furthermore, when you use the downstroke the saw moves slightly right and left in increasing degrees as your hand approaches the wood you are cutting. This means that the slit you cut is wider than the width of the saw.

Though the outward resemblance between Western and Japanese planes is greater than that between the two saws, here again the direction of the stroke is reversed. A Western carpenter cuts on the push, and a Japanese one, on the pull. As in the case of the saws, the pull results in better work. More wooden parts appear in Japanese tools than in Western ones, and in general, the tools are more delicately made and more varied.

114. A rock garden that represents the ultimate in Japanese technique. (Ryōan-ji)

115. A garden with geometrically cut stepping stones.

3. Harmony

Japanese building techniques are not limited to structural ones. In fact, in late years, the unique design methods used in creating our houses have come in for a greater share of attention.

Japanese architectural spatial construction places great weight on a harmony with nature. Since the principal significance in these spatial techniques rests in learning from nature, man has to come to terms with nature's irregularities. A look at only single elements in the natural world, flowers, parts of an animal body, or rock crystals, seems to reveal strict left-right symmetry, but when these same elements are seen en masse as in a group of flowers, the entire animal body, or in mountains and rivers, they are extremely irregular and are possessed of abundant formal freedom. The Japanese eye is aesthetically conscious of the balance within natural irregularity. The word *hachō*, used to express this sort of discordant beauty, has been variously translated by the noted art critic Teiji Itō, who first decided to render it "imperfection" but finding that too close to the literal meaning of the Japanese, hit upon "aversion symmetry." This latter he

discarded in favor of "aesthetic aversion" since he felt the word *hachō* should be translated in such way as to make clear its connection with beauty. Although I agree completely with Itō's idea, because I feel that explaining the meaning of *hachō* in a single English phrase is impossible. I cannot insist that his translation is the only good one.

The ideas of *hachō* reach their highest technical level in Japanese landscape gardening, though caligraphy and flower arranging inter-reacted with gardening to produce the ultimate basic concepts of the style. Though many methodologies purport to set forth the proper techniques for the development of *hachō*, in all of them the first step involves the method called *fuseki*, or initial stone placement as it is used in stone groupings in Japanese gardens. The word, *fuseki*, comes from the game of *go* and indicates the initial placement of stone markers upon the playing board. In common parlance, it has come to mean any preparation for future action when a foundation of actual knowledge about the situation is lacking. The second step in the process is the structural principle of *ten-chi-jin*, or heaven, earth, and man, which is actually a spatialization of the *fuseki* principle. The

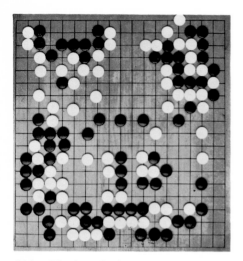

116. Black and white marker stones on a *go* board.

third step is a formalized stage of *ten-chi-jin* which gave birth to the calligraphic forms *shin-gyō-sō*.

4. Fuseki, *the Trump Element*

The game of *go*, a particularly Japanese amusement, has particularly simple rules. Two players using small round black and white flat stones and a wooden board divided into a grid place one stone after another in turn on the board till one player has succeeded in surrounding with his stones more space than his opponent. This is the only basic rule; the one who encloses more space wins. Since a slight mistake in the placement or timing of a single stone greatly influences the later stages of the game, it is imperative to be able to quickly foresee the moves your opponent will make. You must make your own moves conform to what you imagine he will do and work out an over-all system on that basis. This demands the ability to take into consideration many possibilities.

Retracting or moving a stone that has been set is forbidden. When you see that one of your moves is to your own disadvantage, you must simply go on to work out the best possible plan using that ill-placed stone. *Fuseki* is what we call placing your stones with a plan in mind. In other words, it is starting out on the basis of what you imagine future conditions will be, though your real knowledge of that situation may be vague.

In gardening techniques, the *yakumono*, or things with a purpose, are the elements that, like the *fuseki* in the game, are the focal points for action based on an idea of what the future situation will be. Whether these things are trees (*yakumoku*), stones

Setting stepping stones.

117. Placing the first stone.

118. Determine your aim in general, then place the second and third stones.

119. Fill in between the first two stones.

120. Fill in between the other two.

121. When all the stones are in place, it makes no difference which ones were the trump stones.

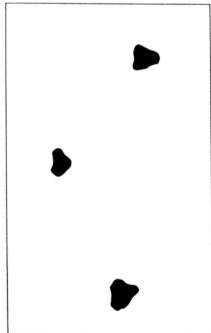

(*yakuseki*), or branches (*yakueda*), their purpose sets them apart from ordinary trees, stones, and branches. Unlike the *go* stones that are always the same size and always either black or white, the *yakumono* have no permanently fixed forms. On the contrary, their significance lies both in their placement and in the process of their changing. Consequently, in many instances, from the finished form of the garden we cannot tell what were the significant early formal elements. This is not an aesthetic of the finished form but a design technique that concentrates on the process of giving birth to the finished forms.

Once again, Teiji Itō has given us a good translation of the concept of *fuseki*. Since the stones called *yakuseki* are the keypoints of the garden design, he first thought he would call them "keystones," but the particular meaning of this word in English convinced him it was inappropriate. He then thought of trumps in a card game. Trumps, though like all the other cards in the deck, are set apart by their function as something special. Although a formative stone or tree in a garden design is essentially like all other stones or trees, its function, arbitrarily imposed as with trumps, makes it something special. With this in mind, Itō decided to term such stones trump stones, and I suppose the way we treat these stones could be called the trump process.

5. Beauty and Function of the Trump Stone

What is the need of trump stones?

Once again we can turn to Itō for an explanation. Factory-produced tiles, all the same shape, look the same in a floor wherever you start laying them. Not so with garden stepping

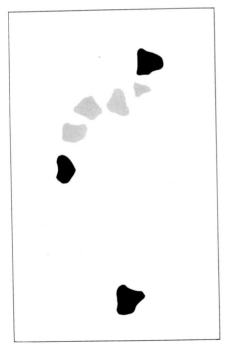 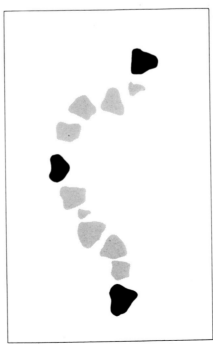 

stones, which must be both beautifully set and easy to walk on. In beauty of setting, the way the stones are joined is the question. In walking convenience, the number of stones, which governs the width of the stride one must take, is the main point. The trump stone is the element that makes it possible to satisfy both these requirements.

For instance, if we set out simply laying one stone after another from one point to another, we will use all the good stones first and run out of suitable ones at the end. If we can buy only the best stones for the whole series, well and good, but that runs into money. For this reason Japanese garden designers and gardeners do not at first set out a definite course for their stepping stones. Before they set a single stone, they establish keypoints, where they set their trump stones. The first may be at the beginning of the path of stones, say in front of the entrance to the garden. The next might be at a spot where the path splits in two directions, and the third at some rising from which the view of the garden is good or at the edge of a pond. These are the hints for the whole course. The gardener sets these trumps first and then uses ordinary stones to fill in the spaces among them. The system prevents any serious loss of harmony. It is impossible with this method to plot out the entire course of all the stepping stones from the beginning. Since the Japanese gardener, or architect, does not begin with a blueprint plan of the entire garden, though he has an image of the completed product, he could not put it down on paper. In other words, the process he will use is set, but no definite plans have been formulated.

6. The Fuseki Concept in Houses

The same idea carries over into Japanese house planning. The carpenter setting out to build an ordinary traditional Japanese house does not use detailed plans. He first uses charcoal to draw on a board the house's vertical and horizontal lines. He next marks the column positions and makes some signs indicating the laying of the beams and the roof. This is all he writes down. The horizontal and vertical lines of the grid give numbers to the columns: a–3 or c–4. The foreman may have an idea about the wall placement and the shelf design in his head from the beginning, but no clearly formulated design is drawn up. Form comes to the building's details as the foundations are laid and the posts and beams put in place. Under the heading "posts" fall both those of structural importance that cannot be moved and those that are merely fixtures added later. Should the client want to change the wall placement the carpenter originally had in mind, the two of them can work out something satisfactory. Following through with our earlier analogy, we might call the structural posts, trump posts, around which spatial planning proceeds in stages.

Although the gradual process is fine in that it prevents any serious mistakes, it fails to suit the modern business of house building, because with it, satisfactory cost estimates and budgets are extremely difficult. The modernization of Japanese society has spelt the modernization of house building and the gradual decline of the traditional system. Nevertheless, the *fuseki* concept is a difficult one to discard. Indeed, some of its better points have been adapted to fit modern house design as a trace of the traditional Japanese way in modern building.

7. The Heaven, Earth, and Man Aesthetic Triangle

The principle of *ten-chi-jin*, heaven, earth, and man, is a method of combining a number of elements to create a certain kind of harmony. In flower arranging and garden stone compositions, the elements have a number of names. It is difficult to explain in English this particularly Japanese kind of expression, but I think we can get a good idea of the meaning of the principle if we regard it as a system in which three different elements create a three-dimensional dynamic harmony. Since no given objects are ever exactly the same, complete left-right symmetry is impossible. We must rely on dynamic equilibrium. Even were complete right-left symmetry possible it would result in a static, not a dynamic, balance.

In terms of the heaven, earth, man principle, the central and tallest of the elements in a dynamically balanced composition

122. A farmhouse that clearly represents the principle of heaven, earth, and man.

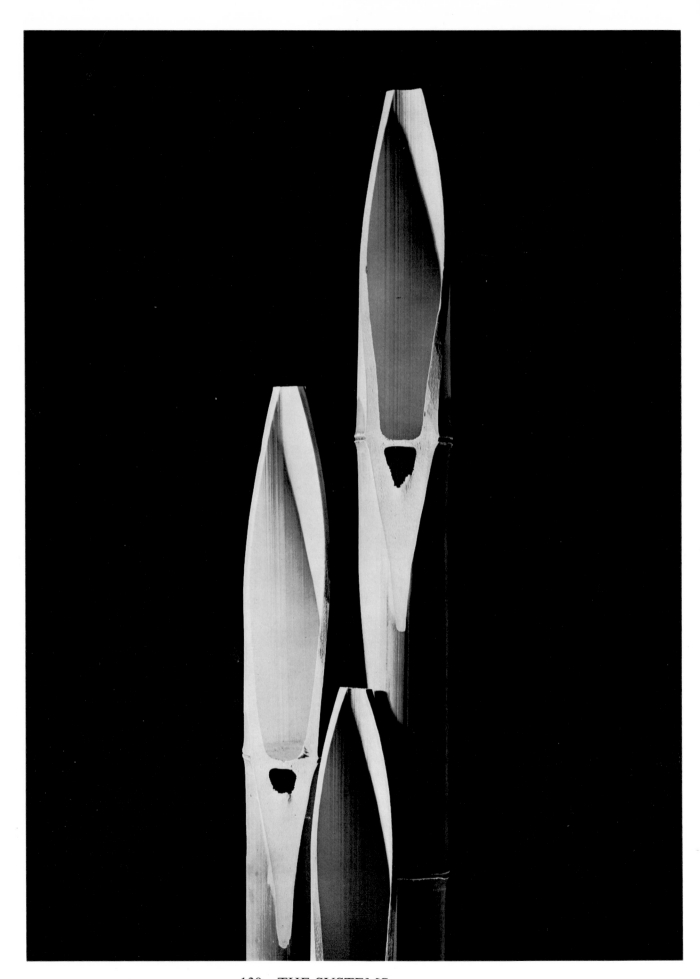

123. Fresh green bamboo cut and arranged this way—the aesthetic triangle—is a symbol of welcoming in the New Year.

is heaven, the ones extending to right and left of the tallest and maintaining the balance are earth and man. The sizes, heights, and front-back placements of these two latter differ slightly, and the three together usually make up an irregular triangular shape. This triangle, the basic form, can be varied by increasing the number of elements to four or five. It makes no difference how many elements are used so long as they are grouped to form the basic irregular triangle. Teiji Itō, feeling that the literal translation of *ten-chi-jin* (heaven, earth, man) was inadequate, preferred his own rendition, "aesthetic triangle."

Ikebana uses so many names for the elements in this harmonious composition that the basic principle itself becomes difficult to understand, but if we examine the flower-arranging theories carefully we see that they are merely variations of the fundamental idea.

Although we are not certain when the triangular aesthetic first came into being, we know that two-element asymmetrical harmony was already a basic ikebana aesthetic by the end of the fifteenth and the beginning of the sixteenth centuries. Deliberate denial of symmetry may seem to a Westerner a destruction of the beautiful, but the Japanese mind, regarding it as a discordant harmony, has raised it to an exalted aesthetic consciousness. In the sixteenth century, when methodologies for garden stone composition were already established, a third element joined the former two-element balance to complete the aesthetic triangle.

Architecture, too, came to make conscious use of the principle. The Katsura Detached Palace and the farmhouses of Shirakawa Village make clear use of right-left asymmetrical placements in which repetitions of the same pattern are avoided. Though, in general, the system is more complicated and difficult to understand, in all cases the importance of additions to the build-

124. The aesthetic triangle in ikebana.

125. A three-stage construction is the basis of the traditional No stage.

ings at later dates is recognized and no completed plan exists at the beginning. It would be nearly impossible to take into account beforehand all of the changes that future needs can work in the parts of a house. The Japanese of old solved the problem of contradictions arising in the old plan and the development of new functional demands by frequent additions to their buildings. The same attitude persists today.

If the basic house were perfectly and accurately symmetrical, additions would destroy the balance. In the heaven, earth, man aesthetic triangle structural principle, however, no final ideal image exists. Forms in buildings based on this principle are always transitional, always incomplete, so that additions of new elements do not greatly alter the over-all shape.

8. Informal Hierarchy

As is sometimes said, our culture knows neither denial nor conquest. This is to say that as styles are born old styles, rather than perish, continue to exist side by side with the new. Unlike the situation in the west, where the birth of the Baroque spelt the death of the Gothic, new styles brought into Japan from abroad took roots here but lived parallel with styles that had already found homes on our soil. This is the reason for the wide variety of styles remaining in Japan today.

We might suppose that such a wealth of variety would invite

126.   A *shin* pavement. All of the stones are close to one another. The balance of the arrangement demands careful thought, but since the design rules are very simple little room remains for individual expression.

127.   A *gyō* pavement. The distance the stones are apart and mutual balance among them are of great importance because the sizes, shapes, and kinds of stone used vary. It is necessary to preserve a total unity.

128.   Stepping stones in the *sō* style. In cases like this, it is possible to select stones from among those on hand and work out an idea using them. Since the individual stones are very far apart, the *sō* style permits an infinite variety of highly individual combinations.

chaos, but in the Japanese mind the principle of informal hierarchy *shin*, *gyō*, and *sō*, puts all in order. These words, *shin*, *gyō*, and *sō*, originally pertaining to ways of writing Chinese characters, may have no conceptual connection with design, but the principle on which they stand applies to traditional Japanese style.

Teiji Itō believes that Akisato Ritoken was the first man to put this principle clearly in writing in connection with landscape gardening. According to Ito, Ritoken's book explicitly uses the words *shin*, *gyō*, and *sō* in the meaning of three variations in garden construction. *Shin*, the most complicated and the one with the most elements, is a formal style, *sō*, the simplest and the one with the least elements is an informal style, and *gyō* is a moderate or semi-formal style. This suggests that if one were to master the *shin* style, he could regard the *gyō* as a variation on the *shin* and would find that the *sō* would become possible of itself. However complicated a Chinese character may be and however numerous its elements, the stroke order used in writing it is fixed. If you learn and use the order as you write a character over and over you will naturally come to see how an informal style of that character should be made. Controlling the number and kinds of elements as well as their placements and patterns makes possible three different styles.

The three ways of laying garden stones in Japanese gardens fit the *shin*, *gyō*, and *sō* pattern. The deciding factors in all three methods are the relations among the stones, the stones' shapes,

133 TECHNIQUES

and the ways the stones are joined together. Closely set geometrically cut stones produce a very formal impression that corresponds to the *shin* style of writing. If geometrically cut stones and natural stones, or all natural stones are set in a more relaxed open pattern, we have something like the *gyō* writing style. When we use all natural stones, we have to set them fairly far apart. This means that the relationships among them become even freer. Patterns set this way resemble the stepping stones we discussed in the section on *fuseki* and correspond to the *sō* way of writing characters. Although the Western mind probably regards this last as a completely separate design, to the Japanese, it is one of the variations of a principle capable of many forms. As the elements in a design decrease in number, the design becomes less subject to explanation, and its content, harder to grasp.

9. *The* Shin, Gyō, *and* Sō *in Architecture*

The tea ceremony springs from an abbreviation of things. The tea house environment should lighten the soul's burden; consequently, it must consciously avoid formality. Its spatial structure must shun symmetry, and its materials should be rustic natural ones that emphasize spiritual relaxation. The tea-house type corresponds to the *sō* style of writing. Though the asymmetry of the tea house is completely free, the whole must prompt a feeling of stability and must reflect the calm that is an essential of the ceremony. Extreme technical proficiency is needed to insure the refined structural equilibrium that must be the end effect of a tea house's lines and surfaces.

The *shoin* style emphasizes a certain ceremonious element within freedom of form, whereas the *sukiya* style, though influenced by the *shoin* style, developed along less rigid lines.

Though the *shoin* recognizes planning freedom within basic

129. A *shoin*-style interior. An elegant and ceremonial design.

130. A *sukiya*-style interior. A design that maintains its dignity but is still relaxing.

131. A tea-house interior. A relaxed design compatible with daily living.

132. Three styles of writing.
(right) The block style used in memorial writings.
(middle) The *gyō* or ordinary style used for letters and other daily purposes.
(left) The *sō* style, a free style used in poetry and whenever the beauty of the letters themselves is a source of pleasure.

Realizing from the earliest times that Chinese characters have considerable aesthetic possibilities, Chinese calligraphers long ago developed various styles of writing. After the art of calligraphy was more or less firmly established, these three styles, completed in about the mid-fourth century, came into Japan, where they continue in wide use even today.

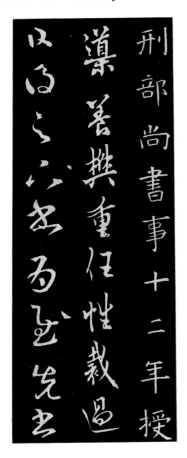

architectural forms, its tendency to cling to fixed partitioning and structural methods makes it correspond closely to the *shin* writing style. The *sukiya* style, though more restrained than the tea-house style, still permits considerable variety in materials and methods. It, therefore, resembles the *gyō* writing style.

From the standpoints of both historical development and of social importance, the *shoin* room is the main front parlor. It is the room with the *tokonoma*, the room where formal affairs take place and where guests are received. For this reason, even today, though the residents' tastes may dictate the inclusion of tea-house- or *sukiya*-style rooms, no pure traditional house can be without a *shoin*. The general thing is for formal and informal rooms to exist together in the same house.

10. Traditional Method Problem Points

The principles of *fuseki*, heaven, earth, and man, and *shin*, *gyō*, and *sō*, are not all there is to beautiful harmony, as the strict current of symmetry that flows through Japanese art clearly indicates. Public aesthetic harmony has become conventionalized, and the design methods involved with it have tended to become rigid. On the other hand, this very setting of method has made the theories behind those methods accessible to everyone and has played a big part in universalizing design. Todays' architects tend to regard the excessively wide currency of the traditional influence as a burden, but the average Japanese still regards powerfully rooted traditional methods as the only real aesthetic harmony.

part four
THE ELEMENTS

11. THE BEAUTY OF THE ELEMENTS

THE HOUSE is finished when construction is over, but its beauty takes many years of living together with and becoming a part of people. Just as in fine brandy, body and flavor in a house take years of aging.

1. Japanese Materials

The traditional Japanese tendency to use completely unfinished materials in their building springs from the idea that with passing years the materials themselves achieve a calm tonal harmony. The sunny splendor of unfinished wood just after a house has been completed is alien to the Japanese personality, but the harmonious luster and dark chestnut color that years of rubbing with dry cloths and years of smoke from the hearth achieve is dear to the Japanese heart. In rooms where only charcoal braziers are used or in rooms in which there is no hearth or brazier, the wood keeps its natural coloration for a while, but as time goes by, cypress and cedar gradually turn the tone of slightly watered good Scotch whiskey. Japanese produced pines, particularly the red pine (*aka-matsu*) and the gum pine (*yani-matsu*) exude their resins to the surface so that the grain appears to float under a limpid reddish brown film. The other main elements, clay walls and *tatami*, also emphasize the natural beauty of the materials.

André Malraux ordered Paris's ancient buildings washed. I was there and saw the Louvre when it was only half brightly cleaned, and I can only say that the venerable old pile looked like an over-painted superannuated beauty. The skin was white, but the vitality of youth was gone. This is not the way the Louvre looked when it was new. The Western fondness for buildings in their original forms is clearly expressed in Le Corbusier's words to the effect that when the cathedrals were white, the people burned with the passion of creativity. He wants us to mentally reconstruct the white that is there under the black that we see on the cathedral walls today. He is not saying with Malraux that one should, therefore, wash the old buildings clean. Though their ideas differ, both Le Corbusier and Malraux demonstrate the same Western enchantment with buildings shining white and bright, an enchantment which the Japanese people have never shared.

139

133. Like carved relief, beautifully weathered and time worn cryptomeria cedar.

134. Many years' smoke from the hearth has blackened the wooden members of this farmhouse interior.

2. Two Kinds of Coloration

The Japanese devotion to unfinished materials got a shaking when, in the sixth century, the aristocrats began actively importing the architectural techniques as well as the culture of the Asian continent. At that time, the Chinese were painting their wooden buildings reds and greens. The Japanese adopted this violent coloration. Chinese-style temples began to go up all over the country, and the number of people studying Chinese literature increased. The columns and beams in the temple were brilliant vermilion, and the robes of the priests were yellows, greens, and purples. Although members of the ruling classes felt the influence of this gaudy splendor in their own daily lives and took to painting parts of their houses in a similar fashion, it had no effect on the lives, garments, or houses of the common people. Chinese notions affected Japanese thought and public ceremonies, particularly religious events, but had no power to change the people's way of living. The method of adopting the foreign was, on the one hand, to recognize the outstanding merit of Chinese culture but, on the other, to distinguish it from the Japanese tradition, the purity of which they refused to adulterate. The result was that while believing in the doctrines of the Buddhism that they took in from China, they held on to their own ancient Shinto teachings. Though public ceremonies connected with the government and memorial services for the dead followed Buddhist ways, the people's everyday life spread out from a Shinto center. Since participation in Buddhism was voluntary, some of its followers were not necessarily enthusiastic, but the Shinto temple was the place where the divinity of the entire village was worshipped. Anyone born in that place automatically belonged to that shrine. The people of the villages were at their most lively in the fall when they held the harvest thanksgiving festival at the local shrine.

The activities of life, birth, thanksgiving, greeting a new year, and marriage were all connected with Shinto, but, since this form of worship barely touched on the questions of what happens to humans once they die, the memorials for the dead alone were left to Buddhism. In everything except the one great question of the inseparability of life and death, the Japanese mind feels no contradiction in belonging to more than one branch of thought. This traditional attitude indeed persists to the present, for no Japanese feels any doubt about simultaneously holding two religious faiths. The two ideas about color, the gaudy and the somber, are a basic indication of this intellectual dichotomy.

135. Temple architecture in a style brought from China.
(Amida Hall, Jōruri-ji, Kyōto)

136. Shrine architecture in an ancient Japanese style.
(Matsushita Shrine, Mie Prefecture)

137. Deep in quiet forests, the Ise Shrine.

3. The Japanese Sense of Color

I believe that the key to the Japanese sense of color lies in the mythological world symbolized by the Ise Shrine. For 1,200 years, the inner santuary of the Ise Shrine, located on the banks of a crystal clear river nearly in the very center of Japan, has been torn down on one site and rebuilt in exact replica on a adjacent second inner shrine site. A visit to the place today rewards the visitor with a prototype of Japanese shrine architecture.

The entire shrine is made of cypress and except for some metal work here and there is completely unornamented, unpainted, planed wood. The simple structure permits no deception. The buildings are brimming with a tension that resembles a refined

144 THE ELEMENTS

theory. When a designer sets out to express only the beauty of natural materials with no painting, he pours all of his being into nature and form. Just as a sculpture made from a single block of pure white marble will permit no mistakes, so a building with no paint covering permits no deceptiveness. It is this kind of plain honesty that stood the Japanese in good stead and remained by them even in the face of the gorgeous and dazzling culture of China. Though the Japanese respected the superlative technical aspects of the Chinese, they could not discard the charm of unfinished materials.

This fondness for unfinished materials also turns up in the process by which Zen thought took form. One of Japan's Zen masterpieces, the rock garden at the Ryōan-ji, consists of a

145 THE BEAUTY OF THE ELEMENTS

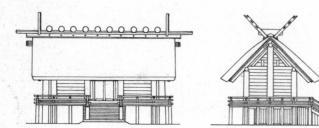

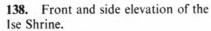

138. Front and side elevation of the Ise Shrine.

139. Main hall of the Ise Shrine. Everything, columns, walls, even hand-rails are unpainted wood in its pristine beauty. Basics of Japanese architecture —a sense of the materials and strict form.

courtyard spread with white gravel and enclosed in a white wall topped with Japanese tile. In the gravel are exquisitely placed a few natural stones and a little moss. The building on the rear side of the garden shows no trace of ever having been painted. In general, when the Japanese took in a style from China, they followed their predecessors' example and painted the temples red and green. In maintenance over the years, gradually only parts of the building were painted, until, finally, the entire thing became a Japanese-style unpainted building. The shift from the painted Chinese to the unpainted Japanese is particularly noticeable in Zen buildings. The reasons for the gradual change to no paint are uncertain.

4. Interior Design

Japanese interior design consists in the nature of the materials used and in their proportions.

The posts used in residences are ordinarily about four inches to a side and are almost without exception square in section. Nearly all Japanese rooms, once again, practically without exception, are floored with either *tatami* mats or with board flooring. For a man to display individuality in designing rooms where the materials and measurements are so rigidly fixed requires that he lay great importance on his choice of woods and on the way he combines all the elements. Since the rooms are not painted, chosing the woods also affects color schemes. The kinds of wood used have an important effect on the symbolic column (*tokobashira*) next to the *tokonoma* and on the large single plank flooring in the *tokonoma*. We see that Japanese interior design involves differences in materials, for instance, in the clay in the walls, in the woods, and in the very grains of these woods, and in the over-all proportional harmony. Because the paper on the *fusuma* and the *fusuma* frames are the only parts of the finished Japanese rooms to have conspicuous color schemes, the whole is calculated to rest the eye by maintaining a color harmony from floor to ceiling.

Houses are put together with such accuracy that it would be impossible to slip a piece of paper between the post and the lintel or between two fusuma. Anyone seeing the component parts of the structure, even after the building is completed, can easily understand the order of assembly.

Two reasons make it impossible to separate Japanese architecture from Japanese interior design. First, since the posts are clearly visible on the interior when the building is completed, interior design must be taken into consideration from the very beginning. In other words, structurally speaking the two are inseparable. Second, there are no curtains, furniture, equipment, or frills in the rooms. Finally, since color-scheme planning demands no particularly attention, there is no such thing as Japanese

149 THE BEAUTY OF THE ELEMENTS

interior design in the Western sense.

5. Japanese Woods

Japan has for many centuries been rich in cryptomeria cedar (*sugi*) and Japanese cypress (*hinoki*), both of which have long served in the main parts of houses. Japanese cypress, considered the finest of woods, is really an outstanding building material. Not only is it hard, but it has a fine subtle grain and a gentle beauty. A house newly built with cypress has an indescribably pleasant odor. The Japanese love the odors of both new cypress and of new *tatami* mats. Cypress is sometimes cut paper thin and used to wrap food. Both cypress and cedar in boards 1/8 inch thick make fine boxes for the lunches used in trips or at the theater. The Japanese are also very fond of the cedar odor imbued in the rice in those lunches.

Cypress is moisture resistant and will not rot easily, even in the foundations of a house. Put in such places where it will be invisible when the house is finished, the cypress may even be knotty without harm. It most certainly matters, however, if the wood is being used in posts or in the horizontal member called a *nageshi*. All of the structural members visible in the finished room must be of good-quality wood and be unscarred with no corners missing. When the carpenters hold the ceremony to mark the erection of the house framework, these members must already be planed and in condition for final use. To protect them until the building is finished, carpenters often wrap them in something like wax paper. The planed wooden surfaces gleam so beautifully that sandpapering them is absolutely unessential. If sandpaper is necessary, the carpenter has not been too skilful. Though, at the very last, the carpenter will remove the sharp corners from the columns and the horizontal members that fit on the columns, their junctures are so accurate that you could not slip a needle between them. Work this fine is always demanded.

Since cypress is much in demand not only for posts and flooring but for traditional Japanese bathtubs, it has gradually become very scarce and, in late years, extremely expensive. A tradition that from many generations indiscriminately demanded certain materials, is now faced with the serious problem of preserving the sources of those materials.

Cryptomeria cedar, second only to cypress in importance to Japanese architecture, comes in a number of qualities from a number of different locales, each of which has dubbed its one type of cedar with an appropriate local name. In beauty of grain and strength two of the most outstanding cedars are Yoshino cedar from Yoshino, in Nara Prefecture, and the slightly blackish Akita cedar from Akita Prefecture. Cedar, though more easily scarred than cypress, has a clearly defined grain and is light enough for use in parts of buildings, such as *shōji* or lattice doors, where movement but not too much structural strength is required and where one wants the grain to be apparent and attractive. Looking at the surface of a piece of cedar we see in the center a dark brown area, called the red, which is particularly beautiful. Just as is the case with cypress straight parallel grain is most highly prized. Knots are held in great distate, because in cedar they are blackish and fall out as years pass. Cypress knots, on the other hand, are a reddish brown and frequently serve as a design motif. In cedar-producing regions one often sees tall trees with all their lower branches cut off. This is done so that the wood will have a perfectly straight grain and be free of knots.

Sometimes for veranda posts we use logs of either cedar or cypress from which we have merely stripped the bark to reveal the beautiful smooth wood surface underneath.

The windswept leaning pines by the seashore are an indispensable element in Japanese scenery, and the carefully trained

141. Towering cypress, the monarch of Japanese building materials. The picture shows a grove where the trees are cultivated to grow perfectly straight and without knots.

twisted pine casts its picturesque shadows in the moonlight in many Japanese gardens, but the woods of these trees are of little architectural importance, because they are usually gnarled and knotty and tend to warp badly. The red pines and larches grown in more sheltered areas are sometimes useful, but though strong they also tend to warp. Nevertheless, they are often found in log form used as beams hidden behind the ceiling. Resin-rich pine, when thoroughly dried and cured for a long time, develops a lovely luster that makes it fine for ornamental shelves or floor boarding in the *tokonoma*. Knotty and irregularly grained pine is most common, because straight-grained varieties are hard to obtain.

Bamboo, together with pine, is vital to the Japanese landscape. Though, more accurately termed a grass than a tree, bamboo cannot fall in the category of lumber, it is essential to the Japanese house.

Bamboo comes in countless varieties. In the spring young shoots begin to grow at the astounding rate of from six inches to a foot a day so that in a few weeks the plants are towering over-head. These young shoots when well boiled and flavored are a favorite seasonal delicacy. The many varieties of the plant produce stalks ranging in diameter from about that of a pencil to four inches. Bamboo fibers are tough and resiliant so that when heated they can be bent in different shapes for use in many parts of the house. Since nails tend to split bamboo lengthwise other methods of joining are essential. Often woven into a square mesh network that takes advantage of its resiliance, bamboo is used for fencing. Sometimes it is lined up to make a ceiling. Split in half, bamboo sometimes provides flooring for porches that jut into gardens, or cut into flat strips it is sometimes woven in a number of patterns for wall and ceiling covering. Since it will not take much of a polish, however, we usually use bamboo only in teahouses or other places in which a tea-house mood is wanted. Cut into very thin strips it is woven into baskets, and in rural areas it continues to play the important roles it has for centuries as door and wall component together with boards and in the traditional straw thatching on farmhouse roofs. In chapter 14 we will discuss the use of lattices of slender bamboo poles used as the wattles for walls.

142. Although a plane was all the carpenter used to finish the column and horizontal wooden member, they gleam as though polished.

143. Among its other functions, bamboo serves in garden screens.

12. POSTS

1. Stone Posts are I type of post used.

For the Japanese people of ancient times the stone was a tangible symbol of the intangible world of the gods. Through stones man could perceive the existence of divinity. Though natural and totally unformed by human hands, divine stones captured the human heart in dim ages long passed.

In 1938, excavations uncovered, in the northeast part of Honshu, the remains of a stone circle with an unknown purpose and dating from an uncertain period. Naturally, it is easy to imagine that the place had a significance similar to that of Stonehenge in England. We can also assume either that it conceals an image of some divinity or that it has some connection with the human dwellings of its time. Whichever line of thought we follow, clearly the vertically towering shafts of stone represent columns. Even so, these, actual architectural columns, or, at least, symbols of architectural columns, never appear again in

144. It may look as if the roofs rest right on stone walls, but the stone sections are actually fences. Japanese architecture relies too heavily on wooden structures ever to use stone walls.

145. Stone used as part of a post
Even the joint is the kind used in
wooden architecture because all the
stone really does is replace the post
part of the wooden post, which
might rot away.

146. A stone circle found in Ōyu,
Akita Prefecture.
Though we can offer no clear explanation of the purpose of the circle, we
suppose it to have been erected during
the period from the New Stone Age to
the early Iron Age.

147. Stonehenge, Salisbury, Wiltshire,
England. Similar stone remains have
turned up in Europe, Southwest Asia,
India, and China.

all later Japanese history. Obviously the Japanese concept of stone stopped at its symbolic meaning and never went on to its use as an architectural material.

Medieval Japanese castles make a totally different use of stone-work from that found in Western castles. It is not that the Japanese were unaware of the common practice of building stone castles or that Japan lacked suitable stone, since they did, after all, build the foundations of their castles of stone. Possibly a firm prejudice against the nature of stone caused them to build only the foundations of that material and, despite technical difficulties, to make the upper structures wooden. Stone, in their eyes, had a symbolic, but not an architectural meaning.

The second type we share

2. Wooden Posts

The ancient Japanese attributed to wood, their very first building material, a divinity different from that which they saw in stone. The two most important Shinto shrines in this country have symbolic posts, each called the *shin-no-mihashira*. The problem of these posts is full of suggestions helpful in understanding the earliest Japanese houses. The *shin-no-mihashira* at the Ise Shrine seems to represent the emperor, himself shrouded in dark primitive shadows. The corresponding thick column at the Izumo Shrine, on the other hand, seems to represent a powerful vision of the people. The post at the Ise Shrine is rather like a pile driven into the earth over which is built the raised-floor inner shrine. It

148. Plans and elevations of the Ise and Izumo Shrines.
The treatment of posts in the two shrines is somewhat different. At Ise, two free-standing ornamental posts remain outside the framework of the building. In the Izumo Shrine, these posts do not exist, but there is a thick column in the center of the building.

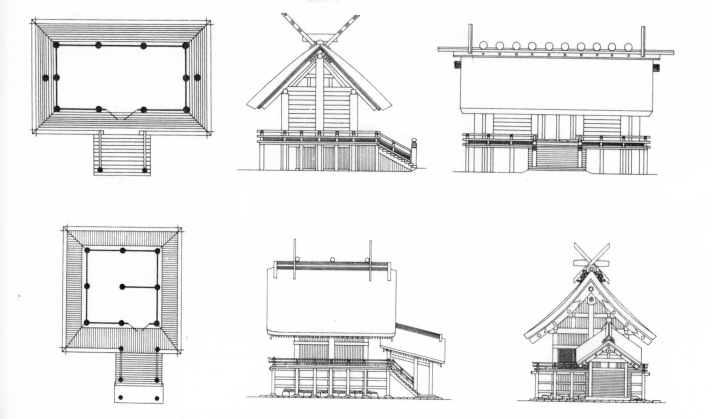

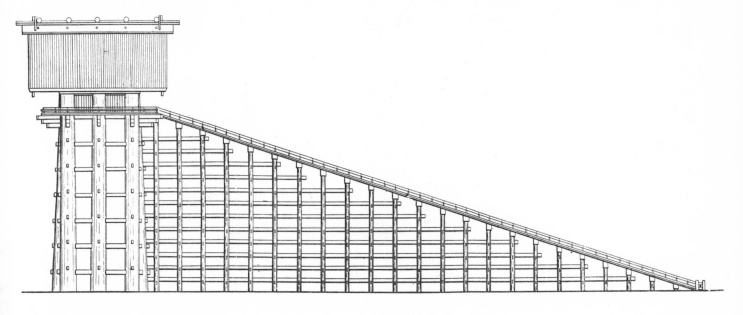

149. Hypothetical reconstruction of the Izumo Shrine (according to Toshio Fukuyama). The building, in this case, would have stood 190 feet off of the ground.

has no structural significance. Although the raised-floor style of the shrine gradually became the *shinden*-style of the mansions of the emperor and the nobility, we are not sure what happened to the *shin-no-mihashira* in the shift. By contrast, the *shin-no-mihashira* in the Izumo Shrine is actually a large structural post in the center of the building. The floor plan of the building resembles the square divided into four equal smaller squares (*ta-no-ji-gata*) that occurs often in farmhouses and may be indeed the prototype of the style. In the center of farmhouse plans, even today, we find a large column called the *daikoku-bashira*. The name links the column with a mythological hero god, Okuni-nushi-no-mikoto, who later became associated with the Buddhist divinity Daikoku, the god of the fields and of wealth. Okuninushi-no-mikoto is traditionally associated with Izumo. By using this very thick column in the middle of both merchants' and farmers' houses the people brought psychologically even closer the popular Daikoku and provided themselves with a support for their faith.

Although the Japanese felt divinity in wood, as well as in stone, stone is permanent and does not decay. Since wood, on the other hand, grows, changes, and finally rots, the people were not afraid to use human processes on it. The bravery and life of the tree as it defies gravity and grows upward to the sun and air distinguishes it from inert stone. The Japanese deified the tree before they turned to it as a building material. From this sense of divinity were born the revered *tokonoma* column and the Daikoku column.

3. Structural Posts

The Japanese building consists of two sections: the framework or the long slender wooden members assembled together, and

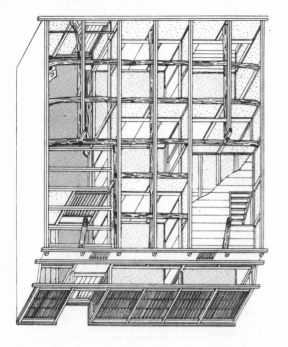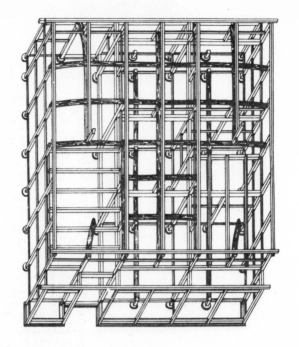

150. A farmhouse framework, the finished structure on the right, and the same with the walls added on the left. It is impossible to tell finishing and structure apart. (Photograph courtesy of the Bijutsu Shuppan-sha, Tōkyō)

the fixtures, the doors, windows, and walls. The English words "framework" and "fixtures" do not always fit the Japanese meaning, however, since what the Japanese mean by framework is only the posts and beams which create a space full of holes and with no partitioning at all. The assembly method is very different from the Western way of combining a number of rectangular columns. In the West the parts corresponding to columns are dispersed, and since they double as wall structure, when you have erected a Western framework, you have necessarily established the placement of the walls. In the Japanese method, even when the floor plan and column placement are completely set, it is not necessarily true that the makeup of the walls is determined. The perfectly square column cross section means that you can attach *fusuma* or wall to it from any direction. The columns double as both structural and finishing material because they are the frames for windows and entrances. When the columns are completely visible in the finished building the structure is called *shin-kabe;* when the columns and beams are hidden within the completed wall the method is called *ōkabe.* Western stud walls finished on both sides fall into the *ōkabe* category.

In general, Japanese architecture uses *ōkabe* only in such places as storehouses or castles where the danger of fire is a more important consideration than in the ordinary home, but even in these instances, the finishing covers the structural elements only on the outside of the building. On the inside the walls are *shin-kabe.* The wall sections are boarded in between the columns and plastered so that the wall itself is always thinner than the column, which therefore protects the corners of the walls. With walls like these, if after the house is finished, the owner should want to alter the floor plan, he can easily knock a wall down here and erect another there without in any way affecting the structure. In this sense, Japanese walls are also a part of the fixtures.

151. From this illustration one can see that the post's function goes beyond that of structural body alone.

A Fourth type del

4. Non-structural Posts

Stat

Even when columns have no structural significance, in the Japanese house, they are still of the same size and square section as the structural columns which they resemble so closely that it is often impossible to tell the two apart. Non-structural columns, the reinforcement value of which is great, serve as part of the *fusuma* frame and prevent the *fusuma* from sliding directly into the wall. They also serve when it is necessary to add a small wall and act as variety formers for the fixtures. The most extreme use of the non-structural column occurs in tea houses, where for the sake of variety, but not to completely partition off the space, a free-standing column is sometimes installed in the middle of the room. Columns used for such purely visual effects are frequently left in their natural state, bark, twists, knots, and all, to become themselves an object of admiration. *Stop*

The so-called *tokobashira*, the column just beside the *tokonoma*, is another example of a formal use of non-structural columns. The *tokobashira*, unlike the *Daikoku-bashira*, does not represent an object of religious faith, but actually symbolizes the exalted nature of the most formal room in the house. It is a status symbol.

The *tokobashira* is one of the columns that make up the

159 POSTS

tokonoma, an ornamental alcove that first came into use in the homes of the upper classes, during the Muromachi period (1338–1573). Such alcoves would be installed on the side of the room away from the garden and may be compared roughly in atmosphere significance to a Western mantlepiece.

Tokobashira made of such extremely hard woods as ebony, black persimmon, mulberry, or maple, are suited to the formal rooms of the *shoin* style. Gentler logs of pine or cedar belong with the more informal atmosphere of the *sukiya* style or the tea houses. Sometimes a piece of bamboo with a diameter of four or five inches might be used as a *tokobashira*, or in other cases, though domestic materials are the rule in Japanese houses, imported ebony or maple from Southeast Asia might be used. Large knots or cracks in unexpected places are highly prized. The popularity of such irregularities brought about the development of artificial ways of controlling the tree's growth to produce them, but even so, the manmade product must look as if nature herself has done the work. Special materials treatment and the pursuit of the novel rather than the beautiful have brought on a decline in design points like these.

152. Non-structural column, a *tokobashira* made of ebony.

13. FLOORS

1. Tatami

An old Japanese saying has it that with wives and *tatami*, the newer, the better. Of course, as far as the wives go, this is I fear only a smart saying that reflects male arrogance, but it is a fact beyond dispute that new *tatami* are definitely the best. The feeling one gets on a hot muggy day by coming home and walking barefoot across *tatami* that are new enough to still retain some of their soft green color belies description. People from other lands who visit this country almost always feel the same way. Perhaps the reason for the pleasant sensation new *tatami* give has something to do with the Japanese climate.

The *tatami* themselves consist of a thin mat of tightly woven rushes on top of a coarser mat about two inches thick of straw tightly bound with cords. The upper mat is sewn to the lower one with twine. They are an ideal flooring in that they are not too soft to walk on but are also not too hard to lie down on. The spring they give resembles that of fine carpeting, but since they have a completely smooth surface they are easier to walk on than carpet. The *tatami* provide us with a surface on which not only to spread pallet-like bedding for sleep, but also on which to just lie down for a nap with nothing under us at all. We put our low dining tables on top of the *tatami* and eat, or we receive guests kneeling on the *tatami*. Flooring they are of course, but *tatami* are also a furniture-like convenient article creating most versatile living spaces.

As the column is the symbolic representation of Japanese residential spaces, so *tatami* are the measuring scale of those spaces. As we have discussed at greater detail in chapter nine, Dimensions, the *tatami* size of three by six feet does not alter radically all over the country. Usually, when we are drawing up a house plan we first determine the number of *tatami* to be used in a given space because this helps us understand the area of the space and judge the functions to which the space can be put. The influence of the three-by-six-foot module extends even to the bath and storage closets where, of course, *tatami* are not used. One of Japan's most outstanding architects, Kenzo Tange, gives the following explanation for his decision to use *tatami* throughout his own home, except in the bath and toilets.

"It is certainly not that I am satisfied to use *tatami* simply because they are a traditional Japanese building material. I used them, even in this modern age of greatly advanced architectural

161

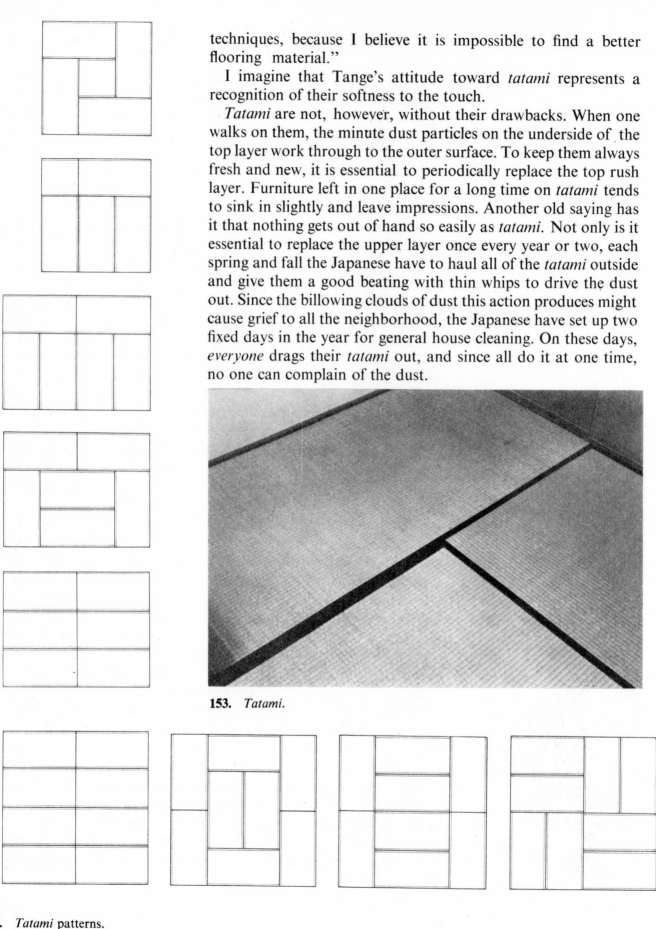

techniques, because I believe it is impossible to find a better flooring material."

I imagine that Tange's attitude toward *tatami* represents a recognition of their softness to the touch.

Tatami are not, however, without their drawbacks. When one walks on them, the minute dust particles on the underside of the top layer work through to the outer surface. To keep them always fresh and new, it is essential to periodically replace the top rush layer. Furniture left in one place for a long time on *tatami* tends to sink in slightly and leave impressions. Another old saying has it that nothing gets out of hand so easily as *tatami*. Not only is it essential to replace the upper layer once every year or two, each spring and fall the Japanese have to haul all of the *tatami* outside and give them a good beating with thin whips to drive the dust out. Since the billowing clouds of dust this action produces might cause grief to all the neighborhood, the Japanese have set up two fixed days in the year for general house cleaning. On these days, *everyone* drags their *tatami* out, and since all do it at one time, no one can complain of the dust.

153. *Tatami.*

154. *Tatami* patterns.
Four-and-one-half-mat room.
Six-mat room.
Eight-mat room.

162   THE ELEMENTS

2. Wooden Flooring

Though *tatami* floor covering occupies the place of honor in Japanese houses, wooden floors, too, get repeated high polishings, and no speck of dust is allowed to remain on them for long. On the garden side of *tatami* rooms, an *engawa*, a wooden-floored veranda, serves as a corridor and as a sort of sunroom. *Shōji* or glass sliding doors, or both, extend all the way to the floor and open wide so that it is possible to go directly to and from the garden. Board flooring is used in the *engawa* because *tatami* are unsuitable for direct contact with either rain or strong sunlight. The boards are generally three inches wide, more than twelve feet long, and of high-quality Japanese cypress. The secret of the high gloss and flawless surface of the board floors lies in the cleanliness-loving Japanese housewife's daily cleaning routine. Once she has seen her husband off to work and sent the children to school, she takes out the broom, sweeps the whole house clean, and then with a tightly wrung-out damp rag wipes all of the furniture and all of the wooden fittings in the house including the *engawa* floor. As the years pass, the floored areas take on a quiet gloss as lovely as that of fine wooden furniture. Not only is the *engawa* floor polished as bright and clean as a table, it actually sometimes serves the purpose of furniture. Friendly callers sit on it as they enjoy the garden. The wife will bring out cups of tea and cakes and put them directly on the floor beside the guest for his refreshment.

In farmhouses, in addition to the ordinary *engawa*, we find a wood floored area, about one third the size of the entire house, which serves the vital function of an intermediate level between the *tatami*-floored rooms and the earthen-floored rooms. On the wooden floor the people of the house not only eat and enjoy family fellowship, they also greet and receive their guests and do various kinds of indoor work. By contrast with the urban house where the *tatami*-floored *cha-no-ma*, or family room, with its adjacent *engawa*, are the centers of domestic living, the farmhouse operates around this wooden-floored area. The farmhouse floor too, like the *engawa*, has been polished over the years to a high gloss and has been made black and shiny by smoke from the hearth in the center of the room. In town houses, where the owner is a commercial man or a small manufacturer, a similar floored room exists, though the size and shape differ from those of the farmhouse rooms. Usage calls for boards about ten inches wide and from four to six feet long in these wooden floored rooms. This divergence from the normal dimension probably reflects the double purpose of the flooring as a lid over a storage space below.

155. Corridor in the Katsura Detached Palace.
This sort of floor with wood grains that are not completely straight are very rare. Time has worn away the wood's soft parts so that the grain stands in bold relief.

3. Earthen Floors

Not only a lack of cement, but also a lack of inclination to use stone paving, result in the use of earthen floors for the entrance-ways and other more or less rough areas where people would enter wearing footwear. Despite the necessity of repeated repairs to prevent the excess humidity in the Japanese climate from reducing earthen floors to nothing but holes, the Japanese generally do not use stone flooring. Even when they do pave the floor the material is tile or ceramics. For instance, in the district west of Kyōto we find a number of houses with the earthen-floor parts paved with large tiles as much as ten inches to a side. The tiles themselves are the result of the same materials and methods used in making Japanese roofing tiles and, indeed, are the same deep, sober charcoal gray. When these tiles are used in the bath the constant wetting they get turns them an intense black that sets off the pale cypress of the bathtub.

Japanese flooring, then, is generally of three types: *tatami*, wood floors, and earthen floors. The *tatami* spaces are for the quieter activities, such as formal reception of guests, sleeping, or study. The floored areas, in addition to being the place where the family might receive its friendly neighbors or callers who just drop in, is also sometimes a place to eat and a place for light work. The traditional dining arrangement is around a low table set on the *tatami*, but lately with the incursion of the use of chairs, city people have taken to using floored rooms and tables and chairs for dining. Though the resulting dining area is not exactly like the farmhouse floored area, the idea behind it is similar to the notion that wooden-floored areas are suitable to light work. The earthen-floored space gets the roughest action. Here the members of the household put on and take off their footwear and store their umbrellas, wet as well as dry. In town houses nowadays the entranceway is floored with concrete or stone, but in rural areas, many houses retain the traditional earthen-floor entranceway where they also store farm tools and process parts of their crops.

156. Farmhouse entrance and earthen-floored area. The people do all sorts of farm and domestic work in this space. Since keeping farm animals under the same roof with the family is none too sanitary, such examples are uncommon. The modern tendency is to cover the earth floor with concrete.

14. WALLS

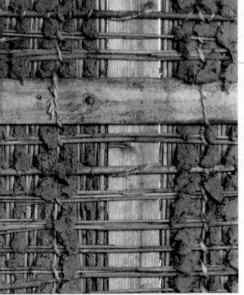

1. Structure

Not only do the Japanese people not sit close to walls, it is considered rude to put a guest in a position where he is against a wall. By contrast, in the West, the chairs are often lined up along the walls, against which everyone sits. The difference in customs springs, I believe, from the difference in the structures of walls in the two areas. The traditional residential interior wall in Japan is made of extremely delicate materials that will not stand leaning on or rough handling.

The main component of the Japanese wall is clay treated with traditional techniques. Although clay permits a certain amount of air passage and is somewhat sound absorbant, it is largely because it permits flat coverage of large areas that the Japanese have used it for many centuries. True, occasionally white plastered walls, to which lime had been added, and stone walls occurred in the past, but both kinds were generally unsuitable to this country, primarily because the humidity of the Japanese climate causes sweating on wall surfaces, sometimes to the alarming extent that the wall looks as if it might be leaking rain.

Once the carpenters have finished erecting the house framework, and put on the roof, the plasterer immediately begins making preparations for the walls. First he attaches horizontal bamboo poles, about pencil thick, in the spaces between columns. He then installs vertical poles of a similar size so as to make a lattice lathwork with a mesh of about one foot. He next adds more bamboo to the mesh to make it finer. He binds the bamboo poles to each other with pieces of fine rope so that they maintain distances apart of about one and one-half inches. He plasters the lathwork with an undercoat of clay to which has been added straw cut into lengths of about two inches. The clay should be freshly dug. He will add water to it and mix it thoroughly. The plastering process involves three coats: the rough undercoat (*shitanuri*), the inner coat, (*nakanuri*), and the finer top coat (*uwanuri*). Each must dry thoroughly before the plasterer may apply the next. The rough bottom coat forms a base for the other coats by filling in the bamboo lathwork. The inner coat requires a little more care because it fills in all the corners and smooths out the bumps and holes. The first two layers of the wall finish what is called the rough wall (*arakabe*), in all of which finely chopped straw is mixed with the clay. For the top finishing coat an even higher grade of clay is needed, and to it the plasterer adds a different

167

(*preceding page*)
157–159. The structure of a clay wall. Process 1: a wattle of slender bamboo and fine straw cord is woven between the columns.
Process 2: three coats of wall covering are applied to the wattle. Since some of the bottom coat oozes through to the other side of the wattle, on that side coating can begin with the middle coat. (*bottom*) Completely dried surface of the bottom layer.

quantity and length of straw depending on the wall or in place of straw, either sand or linen fibers for special effects. Clay for the top coat is usually of a number of varieties from various parts of the country. The natural colors range from yellow to vermilion. Each of the clays of distinct texture or color bears the name of the region from which it comes.

The traditional method of making walls has instilled in the Japanese a definite attitude toward those walls. Once the posts and beams of a Japanese house are up, the whole structure is practically finished, and when the roof is on, the basic spatial

168   THE ELEMENTS

160. Walls of kneaded clay are common throughout the villages of Japan. Though they weather badly, it is possible to repair them over and over again by simply adding coats of clay.

form is complete. As far as the wall placements are concerned, we only need to take the hints offered by the column placements. We are at complete liberty to fill in the space between columns with *shōji*, *fusuma*, or wall. Since walls are non-structural, we regard them as design points, just as we do windows and doors. When a house is finished, should we find a certain wall inconvenient, we can just knock it out and use nothing, *shōji*, or *fusuma* in its place. This is one of the elements that make it possible to add to or renovate a Japanese house in practically any direction.

2. Relationship between Walls and Fusuma

Although the general ceiling height in Japanese houses is eight or nine feet, at a height of six feet from the floor is usually a horizontal wooden member, either a *kamoi* or a *nageshi*, which though resembling a tie beam, actually has no structural significance. Once again, we have complete liberty as to whether we will fill in the spaces above and below that wooden member with wall,

161. Detail of *nageshi* and wall.

162. In some rural areas we find both
the tendency to plaster only storehouses
and the tendency to plaster houses as
well. The design motif of covering
the lower part of the walls in boards
persists even today.

170 THE ELEMENTS

163. A *namako* wall. Tiles set into a coat of plaster resist the weather but are too heavy to stand up under serious earthquakes. Many walls like this remain in the Kurashiki area.

172   THE ELEMENTS

shōji, fusuma, or a combination of these elements. Japanese also consider themselves perfectly free in furniture placement, regardless of whether spaces are divided with wall or *fusuma.* Although, of course, function tells us that it is sensible to put a cupboard or a desk in front of a wall instead of in front of *fusuma,* which serves as a doorway, the Japanese tend to regard such commonsense as beside the point. With no compunction whatsoever, we put our furniture in front of *fusuma,* which we then regard as wall. In fact, since *fusuma* can be opened for a passage when necessary, the tendency is to use them more than wall. The Japanese way of living makes the distinction between wall and *fusuma* vague. We do not often hang pictures on walls in Japan, just as we do not on *fusuma,* because we have the *tokonoma* alcove for that purpose. We look with great distaste on leaning on or driving nails into walls. After all, both *fusuma* of paper and walls of delicate clay are easily damaged.

3. Walls of Other than Clay

Practically everywhere in Japan, clay is easy to come by. This is why it has been so widely used for walls and why even to today, particularly in the northeast of the country, it is still common. In areas where typhoons are an important consideration—western Japan and the Shikoku area—plaster walls and the use of weather boarding on the lower parts of farmhouses are frequent. The Japanese *shikkui,* or plaster, is pure white and similar to what is called plaster in the West. It is made by firing limestone and seashells into lime, and adding fine fibers as reinforcement. It is used on undercoats made of clay with finely chopped straw, or sometimes sand. In addition to interior walls for unimportant rooms and as a waterproof covering for exteriors, it is also used in godowns and castles as fireproofing. The insulating effect of *shikkui* in these cases is similar to that of plaster on wooden walls in the West, though the sound absorbant quality of the Japanese wall is a little better.

In some areas, when strength is the prime point, black tiles, similar to Japanese roofing tiles, are set into the surfaces of the walls. From region to region, the way the tiles are joined varies and creates certain distinctive local patterns. In Kurashiki, for many hundreds of years a famous and rich rice area, a number of old granaries with tile inlaid walls for fire protection still remain. Lined up on either side of a river that flows through the heart of the town, these building recall days long gone by and make a lovely picture reflecting in the river's waters.

15. PARTITIONS

1. *Movable Walls*

Doors hung on hinges are extremely rare in Japanese traditional houses. Aside from the door to the toilet, where space is none too plentiful, or the wooden door that leads to the garden and is not as elegant as other doors, we find almost without exception sliding doors. Most Japanese doors are not covered in wooden boards on both sides but have rather a single thin sheet of wood set into the frame. I think that since in Japanese houses gates, windows, and entranceways all are viewed as structurally and functionally the same, we can class them all under the word partitions. For instance *shōji*, mere frames with thin paper pasted to them, are used in windows under deep eaves and even in entranceway doors despite their frailty in wind and rain. Perhaps we would be safe in calling such partitions movable walls in contrast to true walls. Since such partitions temporarily divide spaces, when closed they act as walls; when open they serve to link two spaces together.

Although all Japanese partitions are structurally weak affairs, they fulfill their function adequately because they agree with the Japanese way of living and with a rule that is clearly represented in a sort of lattice fence-like partition called a *kekkai*, used largely in temples to separate the worshippers' area from the inner sanctuary. The word is little used now, but in the Kyōto region where Japanese residential traditions remain in particularly good preservation we find it applied to another sort of fence-like divider that was used around the table on which merchants handled their cash. This particular *kekkai* was a light, easily carried framework about one foot high and made of wooden strips about one inch square. Though if anyone wanted to step over the *kekkai* nothing would have stopped him it was a clearly understood custom that as long as the barrier was in place, only those connected with the business might enter the area it demarcated.

The *kekkai*, in other words, was the physical object that symbolized the marking off of a space different from all others in the room. We are reminded of the *shimenawa* which designates a holy region in Shinto practice. The difference lies in type. The *kekkai* might vary in appearance, whereas a *shimenawa* is always the same. Moreover, the *kekkai*, while dividing one space from another as a wall might, also prompts intercourse between those on either side. This feeling that, though physically it would be easy, one must not cross something possibly carries over into the nature of all residential partitioning.

2. Controlling Space Sizes

Even when a *fusuma* is closed, the only obstacle is visual. Sounds carry through it with great ease. In the case of *shōji*, all you have to do is stick one finger through the thin rice paper, and privacy is a dead thing. We can see clearly that with such imperfect partitioning methods, without some sort of daily-living rule, the partitions cease to deserve the name. The Japanese express the psychological discrimination between one place and another with things like the *kekkai*, and the theory is applicable to all Japanese partitioning.

Although the sliding door functions exactly as the hinged door in allowing passage to and fro through an opening, conceptually it further functions as a control of size by opening up and closing off spaces. This is certainly a fine method in terms of spatial flexibility, but, as we have already pointed out, it is hampered by certain failings. While fully aware of the bad points, the Japanese have continued to use this method because it suits the post and beam spatial structure of the traditional house. In addition, it is better than a more tightly closed system would be in a hot humid monsoon-affected climate, and, as we must bear in mind, it suits the old Japanese family system in which the father held almost autocratic authority.

3. The Physical Effect of Fusuma and Shōji

One *fusuma* panel weighs about three pounds. It is made of an inner lattice framework of 1/2-inch cedar on to which have been pasted a number of sheets of paper. The outer finish is one large sheet per side of high-quality paper. In traditional *fusuma* there is almost always a picture or pattern of some sort on the outer paper. Glue is applied to the underside of the edges only of the outer finishing sheet so that its central area is not pasted down tight. Around the entire thing goes a frame made of good cedar or cypress either unfinished or painted. The usual domestic *fusuma* is only a very thin 3/4 of an inch thick, whereas those used in temples and other ceremonious places may be an inch thick.

Fusuma are the general kind of partition; *shōji* are used only in rooms requiring natural lighting. The lighting *shōji* give is similar to that of frosted glass. *Fusuma*, with its air pockets between the two sides, are like double curtains, whereas *shōji* are like single curtains. Good quality straight grained cedar (1/4 × 3/4 of an inch) is used to make the *shōji* frame, actually only a large-mesh lattice. The horizontal distances among the lattice

165. *Fusuma* painting. The four panels are wider than those generally used.

slats are all equal. The vertical ones are further limited to ten, five, or three inches in size because *shōji* rice paper comes on rolls ten inches wide. The paper is pasted on from the outside of the *shōji*, except for one small rectangle applied from the inside to make a handhold for opening.

4. Variations in Partitions

Among the many variations in *shōji* patterns, the *nekoma shōji* has a surprisingly ingenious structure. They have a small inset separate panel near the bottom which someone seated Japanese fashion on the floor can lift out for a better view of the garden. The usual *shōji* slat is about one inch thick, but the width of the slat into which the small *shōji* will fit is only 3/4 of an inch. Into

176   THE ELEMENTS

this the carpenter cuts a groove. The small panel will fit without metal fixtures and special tricks. Nothing but friction holds it in place. It will move smoothly and noiselessly and stay in whatever position you choose. Any Japanese carpenter should be able to make this sort of small usually inexpensive panel. Modern homes have them fitted with glass.

Since *shōji* are structurally very delicate, in their place in baths and toilets we use a kind of door called a *mairado*, a framework, roughly 1/2-inch wooden battens, spaced about four inches apart with 1/4-inch thick boards nailed to the back side. This form was used already in the *shoin*-buildings of the Muromachi period.

A special kind of ventilation window, called a *musō-mado*, not much in use now, was once found widely in kitchens and baths where air circulation is important. It employs boards four inches wide and about 1/2-inch thick set in a frame as far apart as the boards are wide. Into the same grooves fit another set of boards the same width. When the second set of boards, which are movable, are directly on top of the first, light and air can pass, but when they are slid one board's width in either direction, it is possible to cut off all light.

166. A variation on *shōji* made by weaving together fine rushes.

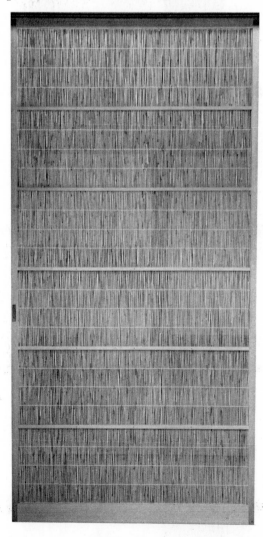

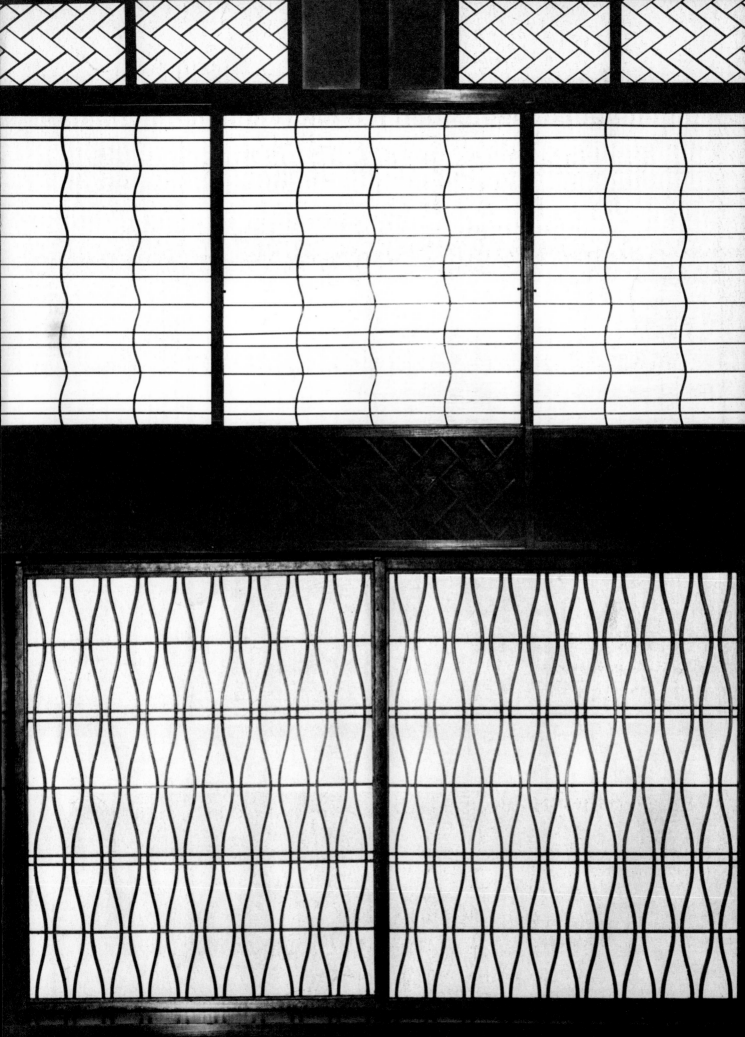

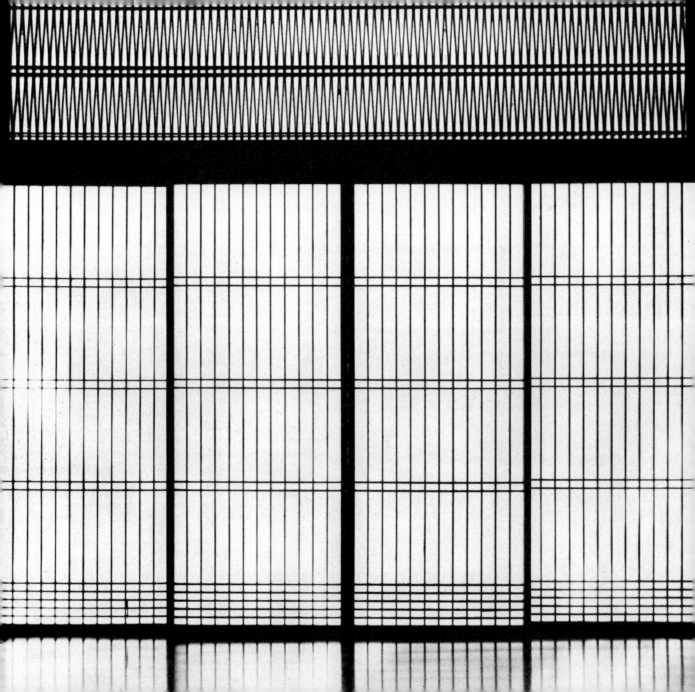

(*Pages*178–183)

167, 168. Ordinary *shōji*. The areas with patterns, the pulls, are papered on the inside of the frame instead of the outside. (Hokke-ji, Nara)

169. *Shōji* designed to afford a view of the garden.

170–174. *Shōji* variations.
All of the *shōji* in illustrations 169 through 174 are from the Sumiya in Kyoto, a famous Tokugawa-period building in the residential style.

175. *Shōji* designed to show only the lower section of a garden(Kohō-an, Nara)

176. *Shōji* used in an entranceway. The boarded lower section protects against splashing rain. The ornament is a Chinese one that shows the famous Buddhist monk Bodhidharma and one of his noted sayings. (Hōrin-ji, Kyoto)

177. A *musō* window

178. *Shōji* used in an entranceway. Since the eaves are deep, the wooden protective panel at the bottom of the *shōji* is very small.

179. Lattices on a house in the mountains. (Takayama)

180. Lattices between the entrance-way and the earthen-floored area.

Takayama

189 PARTITIONS

181. A modern house opening with rails for (from inside out) *shōji*, glass doors, screen doors, and rain shutters.

The lattice door, or *kōshi-do*, used widely for gates and entrance doors from the Edo until the Meiji periods, resembles a *musō-*window with the boards placed closer together. It effectively keeps people out and prevents passersby from seeing into the house. In addition to being used alone, the *kōshi-do* was frequently found in joint use with glass or *shōji* doors. When this happened, the *kōshi-do* was always on the outside, and the sets of boards were frequently fixed in the frame so that they could not be opened and closed.

We also use a number of kinds of other fixed lattices, so many in fact that we have no real standard, except that they all use no top and bottom frames and all of them have horizontal rods midway to hold the vertical lattice in place. Often these lattices use, in place of the usual rods 1/2 inch wide and 1/4 inch deep, larger ones one inch wide and two inches deep. People of the Kyōto region devised a regular pattern for lattices in which every other rod, or every fourth or fifth one, would be raised or lowered out of the normal height. This pattern is no longer widely used, however.

Violent typhoons and biting winter temperatures prompt the Japanese to use rain shutters (*amado*) on all windows except the very smallest ones. The simple construction of these rain shutters consists of a framework, similar to that of glass windows and doors, covered on the outside with 1/4-inch thick boards. They all slide in one groove, and since they are useless in the daylight, they can all be stored in a compartment called a *tobukuro* at one side of the window or door. For ages, the custom has been to close the *amado* with sunset and open them again at dawn. Even today, as one walks down the streets of a Japanese town or village at twilight, he will hear the clack and bang of the *amado* being closed against the night.

All of these doors and windows, the *fusuma*, *shōji*, *mairado*, *amado*, and *musō-mado* are of the sliding variety so that if need be a single opening might use a number of them all on different runner grooves. In fact, in modern homes it is not unusual to see as many as eight or ten tracks on a single opening, each of them carrying a different sort of partition. Lately, taking the hint from the West, Japanese houses have begun to use a grille or lattice-type door in place of the old-fashioned rain shutters.

16. CEILINGS

1. Nearly Ignored

In the Japanese room, where imperfect partitioning makes privacy nearly impossible, the ceiling has not played an important role. In farmhouses, ceilings did not exist and the underside of the roof was exposed just as is. Even when a ceiling was used, it was confined to the room with a *tokonoma* alcove. The same is true of many other rural homes, where the belief is that the smoke rising from the hearth and blackening the exposed wooden beams and straw thatch would make them last longer.

The general ceiling is actually made of very thin boards, about one foot wide, below which are installed horizontal rows of poles. The ceiling boards are cut slightly on a slant at the edges and then merely laid overlapping one another so that air can pass through.

The horizontal timber running around the room at the top of the *fusuma* divides the wall into upper and lower sections and creates a line that tends to keep the eye from traveling upward. Consequently, the ceiling gets little attention. Instances in which the ceiling is the object of conscious design activity are limited to the teahouse, where it is extremely low, and the aristocrat's mansion of the middle-ages, where it is extremely high. In the former case, the ceiling poles are often fine bamboo which gives a natural mood; in the latter the ceiling often features heavy coffering and lacquer and gilt work.

2. Attitude toward Ceilings

In Japanese tradition, a ceiling made of boards attached securely to a firm wooden frame is definitely the exception. The usual structure consists of boards merely lined up properly so that even a rat scurrying about, let alone any human that might venture into the area between ceiling and roof, makes a terrific racket. It is not clear why the Japanese chose so flimsy a ceiling structure. The conceivable notion that since the partitions and walls were none too good at sound baffling and insulation the ceiling need be no better is surely only a negative reason. It is possible that the general use of candle sticks and oil lamps placed on the floor, before the introduction and wide use of the electric light, made unnecessary a sturdy ceiling to support the weight of heavy chandeliers. Some even advance the theory that the Japanese car-

191

penter's extreme dislike of metal nails led him to devise this light ceiling structure that is possible without the offending metal parts. Still, I can accept none of these ideas as the positive answer to the question. As I have noted, the crack-ridden ceiling could not have come about as a way to help keep rooms warm. No, I believe that we should look for the answer, not in functional requirements, but rather in the distinctive nature of the Japanese ceiling itself. I feel that the main causal factor is the need for a ceiling that would not dissipate the light from the flickering lamps placed on the floor, that would give suitable reverberation to the sounds of human voices which *tatami* might tend to baffle, and to create a feeling of delicacy and beauty. Floors, walls, columns, and shelves come in direct contact with human hands; they must bear loads. Their function must exceed that of simply satisfying the needs of mood. Only the ceiling, free of the conditions imposed on the other elements in the room, is free to exercise control over the space's visual and aural effects. When these ceilings were developed the only heating methods were braziers and a sort of sunken hearth (*kotatsu*) around which people sat to get warm. All the people warmed, however, was themselves; no thought was given to heating the entire room.

Later when room heating began to become the fashion, ceiling structures had to change. Though, even now, the way of finishing the ceiling and the materials used have changed little, today's ceiling is sturdier and arranged so that air will not leak through it as easily as it did in former times. After all, walls, *fusuma*, and columns are capable of being heated to a proper temperature to keep a room warm. Only the flimsy holey ceiling presented cause for dissatisfaction and had to be changed.

3. Ceiling Variations

The usual ceiling structure consists of thin cedar ceiling boards, about one foot wide, laid upon small cedar poles about 1 inch square and set approximately one and one half feet apart. The whole thing is actually suspended from the main beams of the strut structure by means of other rods running across the ceiling on its underside and attached to the main beams by means of suspension members called *tsuri-ki*. Since it would be unsightly to join ceiling boards, their lengths must be equal to the full width of the room. As we have said, the edges of the boards, where they will be laid overlapping one another, are cut diagonally for a better fit, but even so, a slight crack is unavoidable. This is why in modern homes, carpenters have abandoned the old method and have taken to nailing the boards up from below. They are still careful, however, to nail on a slant so that the nail heads are invisible.

We always use good straight-grained cedar that will not warp, but when money is no problem and a really fine effect wanted, it is possible to have a single large cedar log cut so that all the boards in the ceiling will bear the same grain pattern. In such cases, if the log is big enough, sometimes the ceiling board widths are increased to two or even three feet. Naturally this runs into money. Cypress is less often used in ceilings than is cedar because its grain is too subtle. In addition to cedar, we also sometimes, though rarely, use paulownia, or horse chestnut. With coffering of from two to three feet across we might use the wood of the zelkova tree, but this kind of ceiling is unsuitable to small rooms because it will not balance with the other dimensions of the other elements.

When we use bamboo for a ceiling we split poles about two inches in diameter and line them up parallel. Since nails will split bamboo, these poles must be secured in place with hemp rope. Should we decide to use bamboo of one inch or less in diameter, we would most often use it unsplit. Sometimes we split large bamboo poles into strips and weave a wicker-work (*ajiro*) ceiling for use largely in teahouses or similar informal spaces.

We have said that some Japanese "ceilings" consist of the bare exposed underside of the roof, but in other instances, the ceiling is made purposely to give just that effect.

For instance, the ceiling of the veranda-sunroom opening onto the garden is often first lined with small logs set in an angle and then covered in boards.

182. A bamboo ceiling in a tea house.

183. A coffered ceiling.
(The so-called White Shoin of the Nishihongan-ji, Kyoto).

195 CEILINGS

184. Classic ceilingless farmhouse.

185. Another ceilingless farmhouse.

197   CEILINGS

186. Underside of a *gasshō* (praying hands) roof.

17. ROOF

1. Straw Thatch

In all likelihood should a visitor to any of Japan's rural villages come upon a surprising amount of bustling activity, it would be re-thatching time when large numbers of the villagers help each other replace old and rotting roofing. So changeable is Japanese weather, that the rethatching must be finished in a day or two. This naturally requires a lot of materials and many hands. When a farmer helps his neighbor, with labor and material, replace the roofing on his house, he can rely on receiving the same assistance when his time comes.

Naturally, since thatching is a fairly specialized task, it is necessary to call on thatchers, who come in a fair number and supervise the plan of work and the placement of the crew doing the thatching. When something very difficult turns up, the professional thatchers handle it.

The thatch roof, still the most common in rural Japan, is similar in many points to those used by natives in Southeast Asia and the South Pacific. The basis of the roof is a set of bamboo poles (about three inches in diameter) tied firmly in a horizontal position to the strut-structure ridge pole. On top of these we lay more slender bamboo poles to make a fairly small-mesh lattice. Next, working from the eaves inward to the ridge pole, we tie large bundles of straw to the bamboo lattice. Once the entire roof is covered, we trim the straw at the eaves edges into graceful curved lines with scissors.

The finished thatch roof made in this way is very similar not only to those in Southeast Asia, but to many in Denmark, Belgium, and other parts of Europe as well. Although straw thatch, as an easy-to-obtain material, makes a roof cool in summer and warm in winter and most suitable to rural village life, it is also highly inflammable. Furthermore, the straw itself tends to rot easily in long rainy periods and after a number of years frequently develops a good crop of moss.

To combat these failings, Japanese farmhouses use a hearth in the main room which puts out sufficient smoke to blacken the underside of the thatch to both protect it from rot and to kill vermin. Although, with a good coat of smoke, a thatch roof may last for 20 or 30 years, the still longer life of the posts and beams and other structural members makes it essential to re-thatch from time to time.

187. Farmhouse with a straw thatch.

188. Tile roof in the Japanese style (*nihon-gawara*).

189. House with a shingle roof.

2. *Shingle Roofing*

In addition to its other faults, the thatch roof is very weak in winds; consequently, in the mountains and on the seashore where winds tend to howl we find the shingle, or *kokera-buki*, roof in preponderance. The style employs many small thin wooden shingles piled one on the other and held in place with horizontal wooden strips or bamboo poles split in half the long way. People often put stones on top of the roof to keep the wind from uprooting the shingles. Thinner than thatch roofs and with a gentler pitch, a shingle roof looks terribly shabby next to a powerful impressive farmhouse with a handsome straw thatched top.

Cypress bark serves as the shingle material for a roofing called

202 THE ELEMENTS

203   ROOFS

(*Pages* 202, 203)

190. Classic style tile roof (*hongawara*).

191. Combination of a classic-style tile roof with straw thatch.

192. Combination Japanese-style tile and thatch roof.

193. An eighteenth-century demon-plate finial—an exaggerated symbol of wealth.

194. Tile kilns arranged in stairsteps up a hillside.

hiwada-buki. Many layers of cypress bark in orderly rows create a thick roof that is not only handsome, but also durable, so durable, in fact, that in ancient times palaces and temples generally used this material, and shrines often persist in doing so today.

3. Tile Roofs

Throughout western Japan and in the large villages and towns of eastern Japan we see many tile roofs. Set in a wave pattern similar to that of Dutch tiles and colored an almost black dark gray by the addition of carbon ink, the so-called Japanese tile or *nihon-gawara* is the most generally used. The classic tile, or *hon-gawara*, used in ancient temples and storehouses, has a cross section that closely resembles those of tiles from Spain or Italy. The method of laying the tile differs little from methods used in Europe. Until very recently, clay was spread on the wooden bed of the roof and the tiles fixed in the clay, but with the development of a small ridge on the underside of the top part of the tile and the addition of thin horizontal strips to the wooden bed on which to hook the tile ridges immovably, the use of clay as a fixing agent died out.

The most distinctive features of Japanese tile roofs are the curved-line pattern (*kara-kusa*) of the eaves ends and the so-called devil plate or *oni-gawara* used to ornament the ends of the roof ridge. In olden days a crest tile (*mon-gawara*) bearing the crest of the family owning the house augmented the *kara-kusa* tracery on the tile ends. Although some of the *mon-gawara* were of very high artistic quality, they are in little use today. The *oni-gawara* is supposed to have originated as a talisman against devils, but in the Edo period they began to become very elaborate and exaggeratedly large and cumbersome, probably because they then served the new purpose of showing off affluence.

The devil-plate evolved literally in the shape of a traditional Japanese devil face, but the name remains even when the plate itself bears only an abstract design. Nowadays, we see them less and less often.

Large houses frequently employed clay garden walls, and to protect these walls from the rains, the owners had them capped in small roofs of the same sort of tiles used on the house roof. Protection, however, was nott he only consideration. The tiles atop the walls prevented the wall from standing too conspicuously in opposition to the house and aesthetically created a sense of connection between the two.

18. FURNITURE

1. Life without Furniture

Perhaps people from the West feel it is impossible to lead a life of any culture in a house without furniture. After all, without a bed, one cannot sleep, and without tables and chairs, he cannot eat. The Japanese, however, using their sitting-on-the-floor system, have managed to preserve the cultural aspects of life with very little that actually resembles furniture. From long ago, the Japanese traditional house has contented itself with a low table, some chests for storage, and a simple shelf on which to read or write.

At meal time, food is placed directly on the low table without any table cloth or covering. For this reason, good woods are essential. Until the Edo period, however, one table for a group of people was less the custom than individual 16-inch square trays with legs. Food was put on the tray in the kitchen, brought to the eating place, and set before the person who was to eat it. Even today, in the country and in Japanese-style inns, these low-legged trays are common. The tray has a ridge about 1-1/2 inches all the way around it so that a number of them can be stacked up for carrying purposes. A trained maid in a good hotel should be able to run upstairs carrying a stack of five or six trays laden with food.

Although the practice of putting cakes and tea for guests directly on the *tatami* with nothing under them at all is dying out, it is not considered particularly rude to do so. In fact, the famous tea ceremony still follows the custom.

Chests are usually made from the wood of the paulownia tree which swells in humid seasons and protects the clothes and things stored inside by not allowing the dampness to pass to them. Old chests are reinforced with often very handsome metal fittings. They are so well made that when a drawer in them is shut air can not leak out, or in. Sometimes considerable strength is needed to open them again. An old custom is to plant a paulownia tree in the garden when a girl child is born. The tree grows fast, and when the girl is ready for marriage, it will be big enough to make her a chest.

Before the War, it was difficult to find anything furniture-like other than these few objects and some utensils and tools in a Japanese house. On the other hand, there were a lot of things in the house that got the sort of use we give furniture. Though *zabuton*, the cushions on which we sit, look like nothing more than cushions, they are used in much the same sense as chairs.

206

195. A single person can easily move all the room's furnishings.

196. *Zabuton*, cushion for sitting on the floor.

197. Low table.

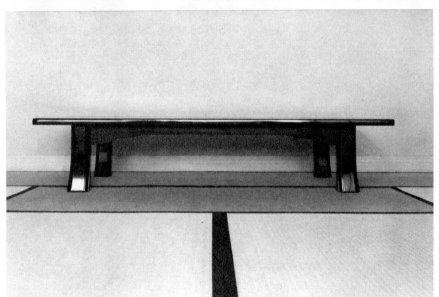

198. Chest, or *tansu* and brazier, or *hibachi*.

207 FURNITURE

The *futon*, or bedding that stays shut away in the closet all day, serves the same purpose as a mattress when we pull it out at night. The *hibachi*, a brazier used for heating, is usually made of ceramics, though some are carved of paulownia wood and lined with copper. Fine white ashes are put into the brazier, and a charcoal fire is kindled in the ash. Since the warmth that a *hibachi* gives only warms the hands, we need the *kotatsu*, a sunken hearth over which is set a low table covered in quilts that hang down on all sides. The members of the family, bundled warmly in many layers of clothing from the waist up, drop their legs into the sunken hearth and cover up with the quilts to trap the warmth and keep their lower halves toasty. Nowadays, the *kotatsu* is not a sunken hearth built into a room but a low ordinary-looking table with a heavily protected electric heat lamp inside. A typically Japanese article of furnishing is the *naga-hibachi*, or long brazier, a combination table, copper lined brazier, and cupboard with drawers. They were widely popular throughout the Edo and into the Meiji period.

2. Easily Moved Furniture

Whether really furniture, or only something used like furniture, everything is made to be carried about easily. Many articles are designed to be piled up on top of each other for easy storage. I suspect that the reason behind this system arises from the way the Japanese use their rooms. Since we may sleep, eat, and receive our guests all in the same room, we require furniture and similar articles that can be quickly brought in and taken away to suit the need of the moment. The opening and closing of *fusuma* and *shōji* work great changes on the simple Japanese interior, and the placement of tables and *zabuton* establish the rhythm of daily life.

Traditional chests are made with draws of a size suitable for holding folded kimono. They usually divide into two or three sections each of which is fitted with handles to enable two adults to carry them anywhere without removing the contents. The traditional tables are made of wood and designed so that the legs fold in for easy storage. The complete lack of metal parts means that the tables last longer. Even now, as night draws on, anyone walking down the street in parts of Japanese cities where old traditions live on, can hear the clack of wood on wood as the lady of the house unfolds her table in preparation for the evening meal. Today we see few of the traditional chests and tables, but the folding-leg system persists in modern tables made of plastic and metal.

3. Furniture's Sign Language

Let us say that a household is expecting an invited guest. Just the right number of *zabuton* are spread in the best room in the house, and, if it is winter, a charcoal fire is glowing in the brazier. If the family is one that respects the old formalities, they will change the picture in the *tokonoma* alcove and select flowers suitable to the season. The *zabuton* all lined up neatly indicate that the space is prepared to receive guests. The number of *zabuton* set out tells how many people are to attend. Their placement tells the guest that all is ready. He can tell from the shape of the ashes in the glowing charcoal fire how long ago the fire was prepared. Without saying a word, through signs like these, the host and his guest communicate. Meticulous consideration of this kind is the keynote of the harmonious pattern that binds together the way a Japanese house is built and the way it is used.

part five
THE COMPOSITION

19. PRINCIPLES

A HOUSE should be beautiful, and there is no reason why beauty should be contrary to function.

As I say this, I realize that some will object that the all-pervading cold of a Japanese house in winter is scarcely functional. I can only agree; certainly the Japanese house is structurally ill suited to general heating, but we must remember that the idea of heating whole rooms develops from the Western pattern of living. The Japanese house suits the traditional Japanese way of life perfectly well. The brazier (*hibachi*) and sunken hearth (*kotatsu*) serve to keep the body warm, and sitting on the *tatami* with legs folded under the body prevents chilling in the feet and lower extremities. Not only does the Japanese house match its natural setting and the Japanese living pattern, it is beautiful precisely because it is where it is. Beauty of form that disregards a way of life turns out finally to be no more than exoticism and complacency, but beauty can be inherited. It is possible to revive the beauty hidden in old things. We younger Japanese complain of the winter cold in our houses because while growing up in the age-old traditions we have also received Western-style educations. Our desire to live warm and comfortable in the winter does not, however, suggest that we are ready to destroy the beauty in our inheritance. A new life order should be able to evoke a new Japanese beauty.

1. A Single Thread

At the beginning of the book, when I mentioned the difference between the Japanese and Western ways of regarding a line that to the eye would seem to permit only one interpretation, I did not explain the reason behind the different attitude. Now, as I begin to discuss the Japanese concept of daily living, I feel it is proper to explain a few such typical native principles.

I have already said that the Japanese use a single piece of string to draw straight and curved lines, both of which they regard as Lines. Westerners, on the other hand, tend to divide lines into the two categories, straight and curved, and to conceive of the two as fundamentally opposed to each other. One of the principles of the Japanese sense of beauty lies in regarding the two kinds of line as harmonious and compatible.

The root of the difference lines not so much in the lines themselves as in the processes by which the lines are drawn. In the

213

199. String and ink-block container.

200. Using the ink line to draw a straight line. Western carpenters use string and chalk in a similar fashion. A skilful application of force to the string with the fingertips lets the carpenter make straight of curved lines as he wishes. Young carpenters can no longer manage this skill.

West, a straight edge is used for straight lines and a compass for curved ones, in most cases, granting of course some exception. The Japanese carpenter, however, uses a *sumitsubo*, a lining device consisting of a roll of string wound in a compartment of a wooden case and attached by one end to a spool. The other end is pulled out of a hole in the case in such a way that the thread passes across a piece of Chinese black ink (*sumi*). When he wants to draw a line on a board or post, the carpenter attaches the free end of the string to one end of the board by means of a small needle, and passing the thread over the ink till it is thoroughly coated, lets enough of it out to match the length of the desired line. With one hand he then pulls the string taut, and with the other takes the mid section and flips it so that it strikes the board and leaves a black line. This is all there is to it, but the distinctive point of the Japanese method lies in the instant when the carpenter gives the string a flip. If at that moment the carpenter applies force with his fingertips and gives the string a twist as he flips it, the string will turn and deviate from the true. Since it is fixed at both ends, it will leave a gentle curved line on the board. The stronger the twist applied to the string, the larger will be the curve. The weaker the twist, the closer the line will be to perfectly straight. Through a sense of the amount of force he is applying alone, the carpenter is able to freely judge the amount of curvature in the finished line. Since he can make either straight or curved lines with a single piece of string, the Japanese carpenter knows that the only dividing point between the two is the instant of the flip of the string when he either does or does not apply extra force with his fingertips.

An application of such a simple principle, the carpenter's piece of string, barely deserves the name "tool," yet many other equally simple methods have come down through the Japanese tradition. The slight bend in a piece of string stretched horizontally serves to determine the line of the eaves end. Sometimes a piece of board is used in place of the string. In other instances, no tools are used, and the bend created by a suspended load is expressed in the curve of the ridge. Though the resulting line is very nearly straight, the eaves and ridge have a slight bend. This and the slightly elevated center of Japanese ceilings are particulaly distinctive features of our traditional carpentry.

2. Simple Forms

The lack of metal parts, adhesives, and paints in the traditional Japanese house means easy dismantling and removal to another site should the occasion ever arise. Only the walls, made of kneaded clay and water, must be destroyed and reapplied when the building goes up again. Since the walls fit exactly against the columns and horizontal wooden members, they cannot be re-

201. An openwork-floor veranda. Notice the simplicity of form used in the handrail.

moved intact. Simplicity of form and a building order completely visible in the finished article—except for the clay walls' inner structure—make dismantling possible, and the demand for highly simplified materials processing and combining makes extremely accurate carpentry essential. This need is the germ from which grew the superb Japanese system of joint details in which everything is firmly held together by wedges alone.

Simplicity is common to all Japanese forms, whether houses, chopsticks, wooden clogs, or kimono. In all these cases, the finished form is not a result of the intended use only, but of the process used in making the article as well. Take for instance staircase handrails or the pulls on *fusuma*. Their forms are always simple, but they are not always completely easy to use. A rounded pull takes more time and trouble to make, and people will always differ in their opinions of how much roundness to give each article. But if the section of the pull is square or circular, anyone can make it. All he need do is decide on the length of the side can make one.

Simply expressed, Japanese forms closely resemble the straight lines and lack of ornament of modern architectural patterns. A direct comparison of the two is impossible since the conditions prevalent in ancient Japan differ radically from those of the present. The ancient Japanese surpassed considerations of functional convenience to seek out formal beauty. Simplicity in modern forms is a result of the industrial production system. Nevertheless, the road is wide open for traditional Japanese simplicity to match and be completely at home with modern design.

215 PRINCIPLES

3. Periodic Repairs

To keep our homes always clean and lovely, we have developed a rather distinctive method. The Japanese house consists of elements that last a long time and others that are less durable but are easy to replace. Columns, beams, and the roof serve unaltered for many years, but *shōji, fusuma, tatami*, all made of paper or grasses, wear out more quickly. From ancient days, the Japanese people have set certain periods when these perishable elements should be replaced. The periods depend on the natures of the materials involved.

Since *shōji* paper gets fairly dirty and full of holes in only six months, it is customary to change it once in the spring and once in the autumn. A little practice, and anyone can repaper the *shōji* repairman.

Fusuma are much more difficult. The many layers of paper in the under structure and the necessity of applying the single outer sheet with no wrinkles and absolutely straight leads most people to leave the ticklish task in the hands of a *fusuma* specialist. Fortunately, it is never necessary to replace the under structure of *fusuma*, the top layer lasts long enough that one change three years is adequate, and the wooden frame around the outer edges is conveniently easy to remove for repairs.

Tatami are made of fine sheets of thoroughly dried rushes fixed to the tops of thick grass mats. It is usually possible to use the top sheet about two years then to turn it over and use the other side for another two. Some people, who are very fond of the green freshness and the delicate odor of grasses that new *tatami* have, change them for that sake every six months.

20. LEVELS

1. Floor Heights and Actions

Because of the customs of putting low tables on the floor and sitting either directly on the *tatami* or on small cushions, the Japanese house maintains a subtle harmony among floor heights and the heights of furniture and fittings. From the type of floor we can tell whether a house is designed for people who wear shoes inside and sleep in beds or for people who go without shoes indoors and sleep on *futon* spread directly on the floor.

Throughout Southeast and East Asia in humid tropical and sub-tropical zones we find many houses elevated off the ground to facilitate air circulation under the floor and to reduce interior humidity. The way of living in these houses requires that the inhabitants remove their footgear at the door and that they always keep the floors clean enough to sleep on. From ancient times, however, Europeans and peoples of the near East have worn their shoes indoors in a living style that calls for tables, chairs, and beds. If the inhabitants go barefoot indoors, chairs and beds are unnecessary. Chairs inspire an active way of living since they make it is easy to sit and rise. In addition, one's line of vision from a chair is fairly high. It is less comfortable to rise from a position seated on the floor; consequently, a life centering on this position tends to be inactive. Furthermore, because rough movements would disturb others seated or lying on the floor, all action tends to be quiet. The low line of vision of people seated on the floor has prompted the Japanese to design their houses carefully to look better from a low position.

2. Japanese-style Levels

Old-fashioned sliding doors in the entrance have lost favor nowadays to doors that open in the Western style because the old ones made a lot of noise when opened and because they require a bothersomely high door sill. When they were used, however, the floor just inside the door was on about the same level as the ground outside. One simply stepped across the high sill to get in.

The entrance hall itself is on two levels; a low tile or concrete section where one removes his shoes or other footwear and a higher *tatami*-covered area on the same level as the other *tatami* rooms on that story. The rise from the paved to the *tatami* section is about a foot and a half, or a little too high for comfort. For

217

this reason, we usually build a wooden step about a foot wide and two feet long two or three inches below the *tatami* level. Since this is still a little high for tying shoestrings or arranging wooden clogs properly, at a still lower level we often set a nicely shaped flat rock. Though the process of removing or putting on footwear requires some fairly complicated maneuvering, the gradual changes of heights from concrete low area through flat stone, wooden step, to *tatami* area make the transition smooth. Even though according to the size and degree of formality of the house we sometimes omit the *tatami* section and use a large wooden floored area the gradual procession of level change is the same.

The *tatami* rooms are always one or two inches higher than the wooden floored corridors and verandas both to prevent dust from coming into the *tatami* rooms and to prevent scrub cloths used on the wooden floors from soiling the *shōji* and *fusuma*. Once we have entered a room, all floors are the same height as, or higher than, the *tatami*. The floor in the closet is the same height as the *tatami*, while that of an abbreviated *tokonoma* alcove may be the same or an inch or two higher. The floor level of a proper *tokonoma* is the highest on any given story. In such a *tokonoma*, where the customary flooring is *tatami*, the level is generally four inches higher than that of the rest of the room. The delicate adjustments

202, 203. Japanese-style room seen from a position seated on the floor. The room from this angle has serenity. (left) Same room seen from a standing position. From this angle, the ceiling, the beauty of which is not visible, seems oppressive.

204. Floor levels gradually rise beginning at the entrance. Each subtle difference in height has significance.

205. In this sketch, famous architect Jörn Utzon expresses his feeling that the Japanese house is built to float on a platform of delicate levels.

of floor level in the Japanese house make it possible to sit on the *tatami* and look out over the garden from a level a foot and one half or two feet above the ground. As one proceeds farther into a Japanese house, gradually, almost imperceptibly, the level of the floor rises, and the design of the house is carefully calculated to create a corresponding elevation of the line of vision.

3. *The Floor and Life in a Japanese House*

Seen from the garden the floor of a Japanese house seems to float about a foot and one half or two feet above the level of the ground. The famous American architectural historian Siegfried Giedeon, in a supplementary chapter on modern architecture in his major work, *Time, Space and Architecture*, comments that one of the most characteristic features of modern architecture is its complicated arrangements of levels. Jörn Utson, who took Le Corbusier's experimental pilotis form and developed it along even bolder lines, in an essay entitled "Podium and Platform," made a number of comments about the Japanese floor. He had just visited this country. According to him all of the floors in a traditional Japanese house are created on top of a delicate platform. Polished and clean as a table, a Japanese floor no more invites being walked on than does a table. Quietly sitting or lounging is more appropriate. The floor, in Utson's description, is actually equal to a piece of furniture and has the same kind of power to attract people as walls in European houses have. In the West people like to stay close to walls; in Japan they like to sit down on the floor. No one really ever thinks of liking to walk on a Japanese floor. For this reason, the basic movements of Japanese life in the house are sitting, lying down, or crawling about.

I know of no better description than Utson's of the nature of the Japanese floor, on which people actually have to walk to some extent but which is essentially treated as a piece of furniture. After all, a floor on which people are supposed to walk around a great deal should be all on one level, not delicately varied as the Japanese floor is.

206. The raised-floor principle applied to a modern Japanese house. The ground level spaces are a relaxation area, (design: Kenzo Tange).

207. In this instance, the ground level is a garden, (design: Kiyonori Kikutake)

208. Here, it is used as a garage, (design: Kiyoyuki Nishihara)

21. DISTINCTIVE JAPANESE SPACES

1. The Veranda (Engawa)

Although the Japanese garden is not nature in a pristine form, it definitely regards artificial elements as unsuitable. It also has a distinct dislike for symmetry and tends always to be made up of discordantly harmonic elements. The space that connects the garden with the inside of the house is the *engawa* which, for want of a better word, we will call a veranda, though it is different in many respects from the verandas popular in the West. I term spaces like the *engawa*, which connect inside and outside, joint spaces.

A highly multi-purpose space, the veranda, because it opens on the garden and is a long narrow wooden-floor space, is used as a corridor, though this is not its original function. In its role as a link between inside and outside it is not exterior space, but it is also not an independent room, and whether it is part of some room or a completely different kind of space remains a vague point.

Since its floor is wooden, it does not matter too much should it be wet in a heavy rainfall. On nice sunny days, it is counted no discourtesy to receive guests whom you know well on the veranda. On sunny winter days, it is a bright warm sunroom where children play and housewives fold and sort their laundry or do their sew-

209. A farmhouse veranda.

221

210. A teahouse veranda.

ing. Sometimes, in case of a sudden downpour, the veranda is a good place to put all the laundry, till it can be hung out again.

Just as the nature of the room is midway between exterior and interior spaces, so the materials used in its construction are a little coarser than those found in other rooms. Round logs are favored for columns and rafters as is wood with a large grain, round thin logs branches,or even bamboo in the ceiling. It is not, however, built independently but exists as a structural extension of the other rooms. It seems, indeed to lean against the *tatami*-floored rooms. Though functionally, spatially, and structurally unlike the other rooms to which it does not seem to really belong, the veranda is an important element in creating the distinctive beauty of a Japanese house. Without it, the house would be much less interesting.

2. Dressing Room and Bath

A Japanese bath, much different from the ordinary Western kind, is deep and not very long. The same hot water is used over and over by all members of a family, but only to warm the body. We always wash *before* we get into the tub, not in the tub itself. Since the washing outside the tub means a great deal of pouring and splashing around, the entire bath must be as waterproof as a shower room. If you get chilly while you are washing, you can rinse off and pop back in the tub to warm up. Your body is clean then, and it is all right for the whole family to use the same water.

The Japanese regard the bath as a great pleasure as well as a hygienic duty, and many people build their bathrooms with large windows with a relaxing and pleasant view of the garden, sometimes specially built for viewing from the bath. All of this care is necessary when you think that we often sit in the bath for a while doing nothing. We need something to look at.

Some baths are all tile or stone, but many others have wall and ceiling coverings of four-inch wide cypress boards. The best tubs, designed to hold water all the time, are also made of cypress.

The Japanese climate and the steam from the bath make it

211. Bathroom with a view of a small garden.

212. Lavatory and dressing room with a view of a small garden.

impossible to comfortably change clothes in the bathroom. To satisfy that need we have a special dressing room adjacent to the bath. We have already mentioned the entrance hall, joint space between the *tatami* rooms and the outside, where one removes his shoes. The dressing room is a similar joint space between the rest of the house, where one generally goes clothed, and the bath, where one is naked. Since the basic function of the room is merely to change clothes, no special equipment is necessary, although in modern homes it is now the custom to include a place where the ladies may repair their faces, and the gentlemen comb their hair, as well as laundry baskets and soap and towel storage shelves.

Urinals and water closets are not put in the bath in Japanese houses. They have special spaces of their own. Lately the trend to include a wash stand, mirror, and medicine cabinet for morning washups and shaving in the dressing room is on the increase, since it is not always convenient to track across the wet bathroom floor simply to slap some cold water on your face and brush your teeth. In general the Japanese bathing facility is more spacious than those in Europe or America.

224 THE COMPOSITION

3. *The* Tsugi-no-ma, *an Ante-room*

A Japanese house floor plan often reveals a small room, adjacent to a large *tatami* room, that though really a corridor-like space is floored with *tatami* and partitioned with *shōji* or *fusuma*. This is the place for a wide variety of preparations for activities that are to take place in the more important larger room.

For instance, if a guest is seated with his back to the *tokonoma* with his face turned toward the garden, to bring in tea and cakes from the veranda, would block his view, whereas opening the *fusuma* between the ante-room and the main room and bringing in refreshments that way causes no disturbance at all. Usually this ante-room, *tsugi-no-ma*, is small and contains only a single row of *tatami* mats lined up in a straight line. It serves as a place to temporarily hang a visitors coat or as a storage room for all of the *zabuton* cushions. When a guest is staying overnight, he will sleep in the room with the *tokonoma* and use the ante-room to change clothes. In some large houses the ante-room is placed so that it can serve two larger rooms. When a house is not large enough to permit the luxury of a *tsugi-no-ma*, one of two large rooms will serve the same function for the large room on which it opens.

Just as the thoughtful host has a small pavilion built in his gardens where a last minute check can be made of the refreshments from the main house before he offers them to his guests, so he has a *tsugi-no-ma* where similar checks can be made before offering refreshments to guests received indoors.

The nature of the *tsugi-no-ma* as joint space between the more important room and other rooms, say the corridor, dictates an unobtrusive freshness in its decor.

213. A room with no existence independent of other rooms, the *tsugi-no-ma* is an extension of the main room when the *fusuma* are open.

22. CONTEMPORARY JAPANESE HOUSES

I think I have explained all of the really important points in the Japanese house, but in conclusion, I would like to give you a list of requisites by which it is possible to say whether a given room is really Japanese or whether it smacks of the foreign. The first half of the list of entries are absolute essentials. Without any one of them the truly Japanese nature is lost. The latter half contains a number of elements which add up to a purer Japanese style. The more of them the better. A room that meets all fourteen of these conditions gets full marks as completely Japanese in style.

ESSENTIALS

1. All unpainted wood. We usually avoid stain and clear lacquer as well, though not as strictly as we exclude paint.
2. *Tatami*-covered floor. A single part of the room may be floored with boards.
3. All openings through which one enters or exits fitted with sliding *shōji* or *fusuma*.
4. All posts square and all wooden members exposed.
5. Eaves deep, two to four feet, with exposed rafters.
6. All furniture suited to sitting directly on the floor.

SUPPLEMENTARIES

7. With the exception of the *tokonoma* post, all wood either Japanese cryptomeria cedar, cypress, or pine.
8. All walls, clay, sand finished, or plaster. It is acceptable to use cloth, or cloth-like Japanese wallpapers, or traditional Japanese paper.
9. Ceiling boards should be wide (one to one and a half feet).
10. The special Japanese lintel (*kamoi*) and horizontal members attached to the outside of the columns (*nageshi*) should be used.
11. When possible a *tokonoma* should be used because it provides a good place for displaying scrolls and ornaments.
12. All interior lines should be straight, and all excess ornament avoided.
13. All levels should be carefully calculated. The *tatami* should be one and one half inches higher than the corridor floor. The floor of the *tokonoma* should be the same as, or a little higher than the room floor.
14. Lighting fixtures should be absent or made of wood and

226

paper. Those that are round in shape or have plated metal parts, and crystal chandeliers are not traditional Japanese.

The following photographs will illustrate what I mean.

Contemporary Japanese Houses

Although the houses going up today in this country are many and various, purely Japanese houses or pure copies of Western houses are very rare, because both the people and the architects adopt the elastic attitude of "Let's keep what is good, whether its old or not, but lets add as many good new things as possible."

I selected as many candidates for inclusion in the book as I could find and as I thought would adequately illustrate the present elastic attitude toward building. I first put the houses into groups according to general type, and then I selected the ones whose designs best expressed the salient points I wanted to illustrate.

Since I deal with those salient points in detail when we get to the actual examples, here I will simply say a word about the general groups. Unfortunately we still lack sufficient statistical data to supply us with a real scientific backing for the groupings I made.

In some instances, I divided the houses into concrete and wooden ones, in some, into those that use the Japanese space dividing concepts and some that divide into Western-style rooms, and in others I contrasted those that use *fusuma* and *tatami* in different ways.

I realize that this method inevitably involves a lot of over-lapping, but since no grouping would really show the elasticity of the Japanese attitude as clearly as is necessary, I have not been too strict in adhering to groups. Nevertheless, I feel that I have been able to illustrate and amplify the theme of the book.

1. Minimum House
designed by the author (1958).

(*right*)
214. Under the elevated floor are spread small stones in a style that re-calls ancient Japanese shrines. The floors and columns are concrete and the walls plastered for fire-prevention reasons.

Westernization is the most pronounced feature of the living pattern of contemporary younger Japanese. A close look at today's houses, however, reveals many traditional Japanese traits persisting in the midst of newer customs.

The reader will forgive me for including my own house in my examples, but a number of architectural magazines have seen fit to publish the building, and I feel it is to the point because it observes all of the essential conditions we discussed in our check-list of Japanese elements. Somehow or other, the general mood of the building is very Japanese.

All of the wood is completely unpainted, and the concrete itself is unfinished. Rush mats cover the floors. The doors are sliding ones, the post are square in section, and the eaves are deep.

The first level underfloor section is a garage, and the living room boasts a telephone, whiskey bottles on the shelf, a sofa bed, a table with chair and a typewriter. In other words, my intention in the design was to use this sort of form in a way that would harmonize with the modern way of life of the younger group of Japanese people.

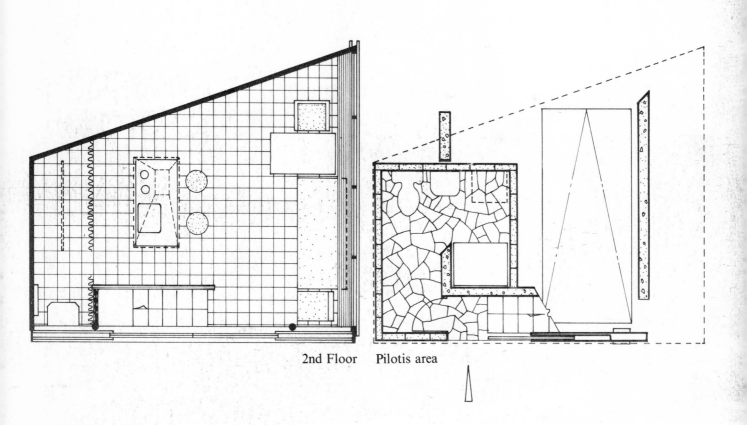

2nd Floor   Pilotis area

215. Rush mats cover the floor; the wall finishing is plywood. The window on the right has sliding panels. The ceiling is exposed rafters with cedar boards.

(*right*)

216. A photograph of the same room, taken in summer. It is a little hard to realize the actual scale of the room from the picture. The high point of the ceiling is about twice the height of an average man. From the foot of the stairs, that height is four times that of an average man. The stairwell wall is unfinished concrete, and the handrail and diagonal brace are cypress logs.

2. *The Sky House*
designed by Kiyonori Kikutake (1958).

(right)

217. Four massive unfinished concrete pillars support the house on a site that slopes away to the south. The rain shutters on the terrace around the house operate on the *musō*-window principle.

218. This view of the southeast corner makes the entrance arrangement clear. The road level is halfway between the house entrance and the garden below. Descend half the staircase, and you are in the garden. Mount half the staircase, and you are at the front door.

Another architect's house, this is an extreme example of the elevated floor. Although many people are prone to regard this as dubious Japanese in style, I feel that the open floor plan clearly indicates the building's national character. As I have mentioned, the Japanese house is a single space imperfectly partitioned with *fusuma* and the like. Unity of space is obvious in this house, where only single-leaf screens and furniture partition one large space.

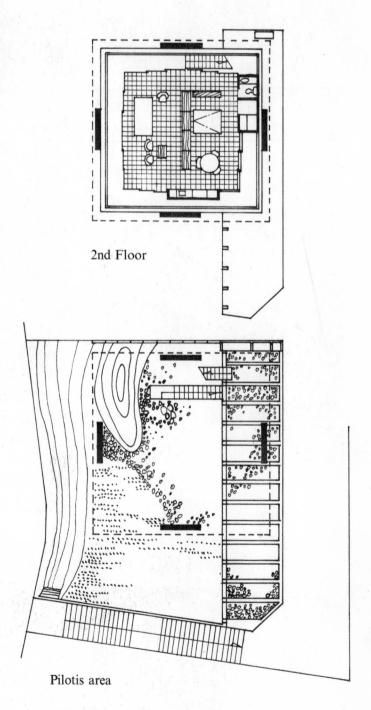

2nd Floor

Pilotis area

219. Although the floor is covered in Western plastic tile, the large platform on the left serves many of the functions of ordinary *tatami*. One might use it as a bench, or sit on it cross-legged in the Japanese fashion. Notice that ashtrays and cups are set directly on the platform.

220. Bamboo curtains hang at the glass doors separating the interior (left) from the terrace (right).

3. Residence

designed by Kenzō Tange (1953).

This house has received praise as an outstanding piece of modern architecture that makes ample use of the good points of the Japanese residential tradition. The architect's own home, it is the only example of residential design ever done by Tange, who is primarily an architect of public buildings and an urban designer. Aside from its design excellence, the house is historically important because it pointed the way for future developments in Japanese residential building at a time after the War when everything was still in a turmoil.

The pilotis, the most distinctive feature of the house, is not merely open space. It serves as a place to hang laundry, for the children to play on rainy days, and for the family to enjoy the evening cool or to sunbathe. The balcony and deep overhang on the south side of the upper level link the interior of the house with the garden. Apart from the bath and toilet, nearly all of the interior floors are *tatami*, which, treated as merely a floor finishing, are made to bear chairs or tables, or whatever else the residents want to put on them. The windows use *shōji* and sliding glass doors but no rain shutters. All of the transoms over the *fusuma* are filled with glass for a very bright interior.

2nd Floor

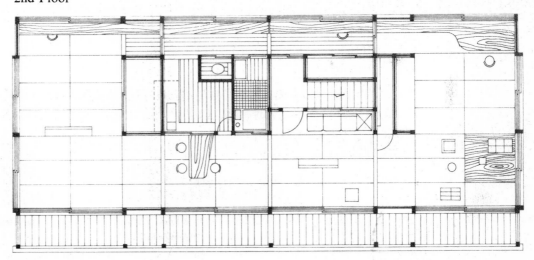

Pilotis area

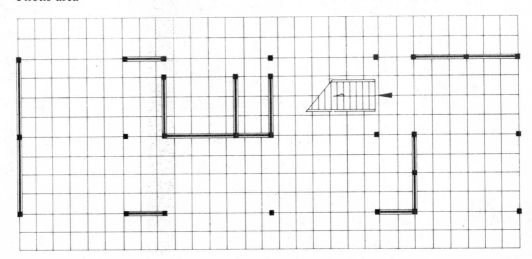

236   THE COMPOSITION

221. This view from the south clearly shows the pilotis.

222. Closeup of the south side. Only the double joists are a Western touch.

223. The terrace, balcony, and garden are in effect all one space. The hillocks in the background take the place of a fence.

224. View of the garden from inside the house. The large gingko trees on the far side of the garden effectively shield the house from the road.

237 CONTEMPORARY JAPANESE HOUSES

(*left*)

225. The room on the far east is the most formal and serves as a reading and reception room. The painting on the wall is modern calligraphy. Isamu Noguchi designed the lighting fixture using the traditional paper lanterns as a hint.

226. Lattices in the east and west walls protect from direct sunlight.

227. The board insets in the *tatami* floor are for chairs. The walls are lauan plywood.

228. View to the west. The mid-ground room opens on the kitchen and entrance. In the distance is the bedroom. The family eats seated in Japanese-style chairs, but when guests come, everyone sits directly on the *tatami*.

239 CONTEMPORARY JAPANESE HOUSES

4. The Karasuyama House
designed by Shin Takasugi (1965).

(*right*)
229. The *tatami* in this room are of a not-too-often-employed borderless variety. Because the edges must be bent evenly, the type is considered hard to make. The opening is fitted with eight runners for glass windows, screens, and rain shutters.

This extremely refreshing and frank house consists of a large room with a terrace running its full width and a smaller room on the side away from the terrace. The big room is just that, a big room with no particular function but one that serves for daily activities, meals, and entertaining. The multiple functionality of even the smaller room, which is a dressing room, a work room, and a sleeping area, prevents it from being named anything but "smaller room." The house is a good example of the Japanese method of concentrating on the size and combination of the spaces rather than on their functions.

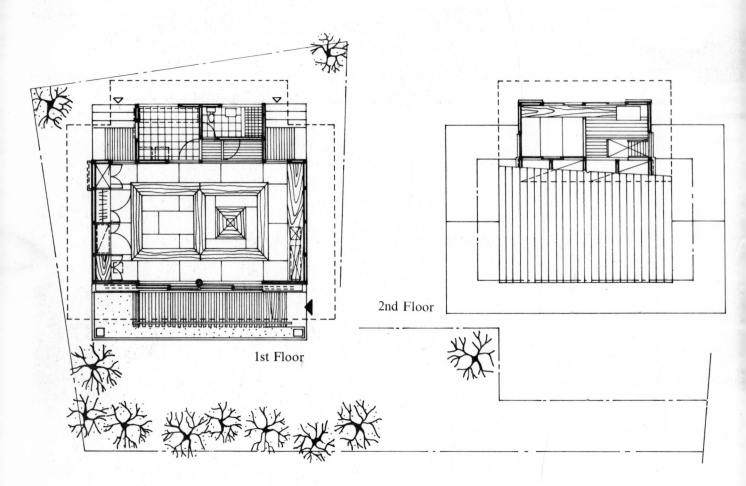

1st Floor

2nd Floor

241 CONTEMPORARY JAPANESE HOUSES

(*left*)
230. View from the terrace to the *shōji* on the opposite side. The large nearly square *shōji* grid is currently fashionable.

231. This view toward the terrace from the inner side of the large room gives a good idea of the ceiling with its four-inch boards.

232. The large pit, resembling a *kotatsu*, in one end of the room contains a table that rises to floor level. This represents a combination of the age-old Japanese tradition of receiving guests seated on the *tatami* and of an improvement whereby it is unnecessary to kneel in the somewhat uncomfortable traditional fashion.

233. The numerous built-in cupboards and closets in the smaller room make it possible to have all of the modern conveniences stored away and still continue the traditional furnitureless way of life.

234. The Japanese cypress terrace is quite high off of the ground level.

5. *A House with an Earthen floor Section*
designed by Kazuo Shinohara (1963).

Removed considerably from town and more of a villa than an
ordinary dwelling, this house exhibits some unusual features.
Half of the interior is floored with *tatami* and half with earth. The
doors are board sliding doors like those used in farmhouses. I
dare say, the client wanted to experience something of the real
rural-village way of life.

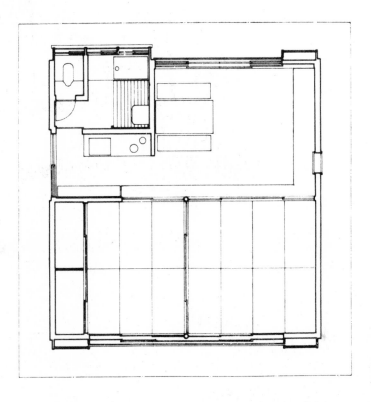

235. Exterior and interior walls are coated in white plaster. Plastering over the beams and the posts is a method used in traditional godowns.

236. Only the rain-shutter compartments on either side of the *shōji* contrast wood textures with the rest of the house's whiteness.

(*right*)
237. The *fusuma* and *shōji* between the earthen-floor section and the *tatami* section have been removed for this photograph. Use of *shōji* for ventilation in the transoms is popular in modern homes.

238. The paper on the *fusuma* covers the frames and merely indents at the pulls which use no wooden parts. This is an innovation rather than a traditional method.

246   THE COMPOSITION

239, 240. Dining room on the right; kitchen on the left. The gas range and exhaust hood are, needless to say, not traditional.

(*right*)
241. No door divides the dining room from the kitchen. A skylight is visible in the kitchen ceiling.

6. *Mr. T's Residence*
designed by the Rengō Sekkei Co. (1962).

The plan may be a little difficult to understand. The central part has something of the personality of a passageway, serving as an approach to all the other rooms. The board-floored room in the center of the building is the most distinctive feature of the house. It contains a hearth with a traditional pole for suspending the kettle over the charcoal fire. All of the other rooms around the central one enjoy a high degree of functional freedom.

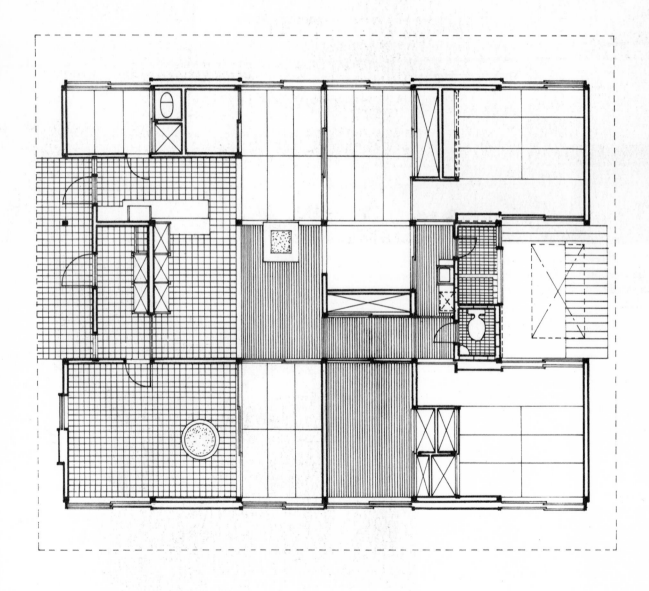

242. East side. Two bedrooms flank
the terrace. The cypress boards are
painted with a translucent persimmon
juice.

243. Inner garden.

(*left*)
244. The room in the foreground is the family room; the board-floored room and its hearth are visible beyond.

245. The dining area is floored with tile and uses a Western table and stools.

246. View toward the bedroom on the north. Part of the floor is a single zelkova plank.

7. Twin Houses
designed by the author (1964).

(*right*)
247. On the right of the flagstone floor is the entrance to the house. Beyond the *shōji* on the left is the terrace. The *tatami* room straight ahead serves for receiving guests, eating, and sleeping.

Though the sites are somewhat far apart, Mr. Yamanari's and Mr. Iwanami's houses were designed at the same time with approximately the same methods.

The stone pavement that continues from the outside through the entrance hall and to the terrace is the most distinguishing feature of the Yamanari house. A staircase leads to the second floor from the stone floored area, which is treated exactly like the earth-floored space in a farmhouse. We used stones instead of earth, which is ill suited to town houses.

The free-standing concrete columns on the terrace of the Iwanami house prevent typhoons from ripping off the six-foot-deep eaves. Wooden posts would have rotted quickly.

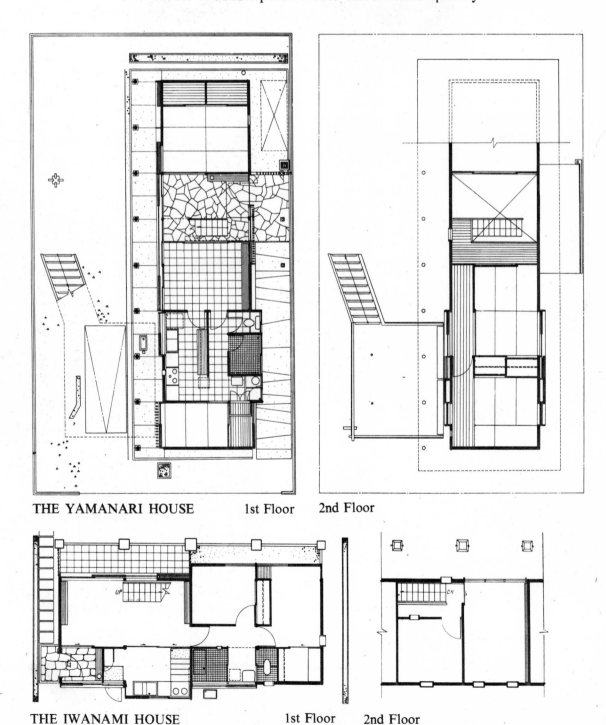

THE YAMANARI HOUSE   1st Floor   2nd Floor

THE IWANAMI HOUSE   1st Floor   2nd Floor

255 CONTEMPORARY JAPANESE HOUSES

248. Lattices in the entrance prevent passersby from seeing in.

249. The dining room uses Western table and chairs and Japanese *shōji*, beyond which is the garden.

250. Looking down on the entrance hall from the open staircase. The design of the lighting fixture is based on the shape of Japanese spools.

256 THE COMPOSITION

257 CONTEMPORARY JAPANESE HOUSES

251. Five concrete columns support the eaves over the Iwanami house terrace. Five is considered a lucky number in this country.

252. The terrace ceiling is unfinished cypress boards. The steel chain hanging from the end of the eave takes the place of a drain. Rain water runs from the roof down the chain to a place prepared below.

8. *A White House*
designed by Kazuo Shinohara (1967).

Japanese traditions, taken apart then recombined in line with modern ideas can give birth to bright new theories. Since the Japanese tradition is possessed of distinctive forms, in the reconstructed design we are likely to find symbolized parts. Shinohara's White House is a good example. The *tatami* way of living is conspicuous by its complete absence. The whole house follows the Western chair, table, and bed philosophy, but the furniture itself is more symbolic than functional. With just the facilities we see in the photographs, daily living is likely to be inconvenient. Japanese tradition rejects disrupting a living pattern for the sake of convenience.

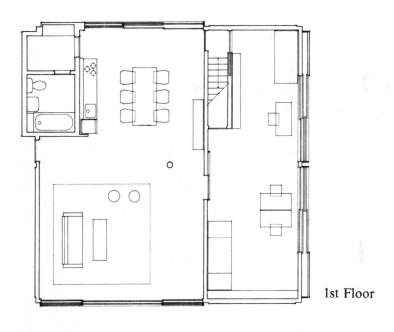

1st Floor

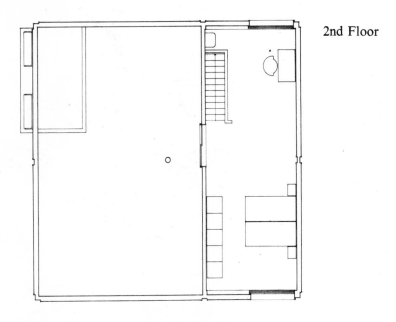

2nd Floor

253. The tiles and plaster·are traditional.

254. The symbolism of the space is based on a Japanese concept.

255. Only the *shōji* and the stools could becalled Japanese design.

256. The second-floor bedroom has a skylight in the ceiling.

257. The only chest in the bedroom is an old-fashioned Japanese one.

9. *A Earth House*
designed by Kazuo Shinohara (1967).

This extreme case of spatial symbolization is made up of an underground section and a section above ground. The underground part houses the bedroom because the act of sleeping requires a quiet space. The above ground section contains the dining and working areas.

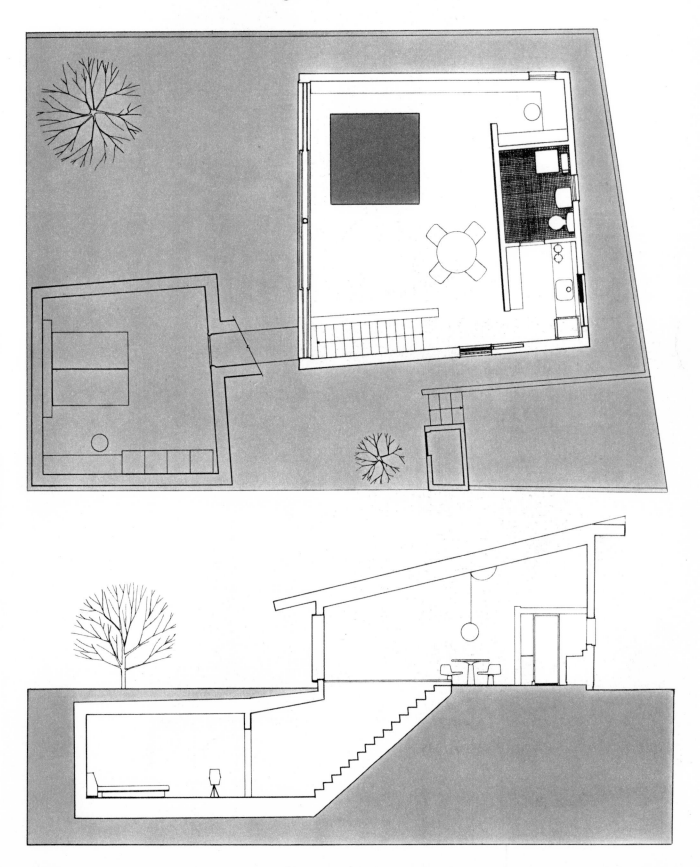

(*left*)

258. The ladder symbolizes steps leading to the top of the platform. The table and chairs symbolize spaces where one does handwork. The sleeping quarters on top of the platform are possibly for the occasional overnight guest.

259. The irregular pitch of the roof which covers a nearly square plan probably results from the need to accommodate the box-like platform in the living room.

260. The low platform represents the kind of lounging and lying down possible on *tatami*.

(*following page*)

261. Table and chairs, a platform, and a ladder in the above-ground section.

262. The floor is entirely covered with pounded earth.

CONCLUSION

I have intended in this book to give the person who has never visited Japan an idea of the daily-living patterns that are a part of the Japanese tradition and of the house which those patterns have brought into being. In the process, I learned that there are things that I, a Japanese adult, and many others like me, do not know about Japan. This is particularly true among the current younger generations who maintain a number of mistaken ideas about their homeland. I find it very strange that until now Japan has produced no books about the Japanese house and the way we live in it. Although I wanted largely to inform people of other countries, now that I look back I feel that my book could be a valuable source of information for Japanese young people too.

The Japanese house is today changing greatly as is the traditional way of life, because we feel that both contradict our modern way of thinking. The old house harmonized wonderfully with living in an age of less sophisticated scientific developments, but with the growing use of domestic appliances and as newer, better building materials appear on the scene, our thinking about houses has become confused. I am sure that if we are to find an order that will return harmony to our contemporary way of living we must reexamine the significance of old things.

It is important that I have been able to write this book at a point in time when, although the face of Japan is rapidly changing, many of our traditional things remain with us.

BIBLIOGRAPHY

IN ENGLISH

BENEDICT, RUTH. *The Chrysanthemum and the Sword; Patterns of Japanese Culture*, Boston, 1946, Hougton Mifflin Co.

BLASER, WERNER. *Temple and Teahouse in Japan*, Tokyo, 1955, Sanseido

CARVER, NORMAN F. JR. *Form and Space of Japanese Architecture*, Tokyo, 1955, Shōkoku-sha

DEXLER, ARTHUR. *The Architecture of Japan*, New York, 1955, The Museum of Modern Art

ENGEL, HEINRICH. *The Japanese House; A Tradition for Contemporary Architecture*, Tokyo, 1966, Tuttle

HAMAGUCHI, RYŪICHI. "A Study of Sukiya Artists," *Japan Architect*, June 1956, Tokyo, Shin Kenchiku-sha

ISHIMOTO, KIYOKO and TATSUO. *The Japanese House, Its Interior and Exterior*, New York, 1963, Crown Publishers

KINOSHITA, MASAO. *Japanese Architecture, Sukiya*, Tokyo, 1965, Shōkoku-sha

KIRBY, JOHN B. JR. *From Castle to Teahouse; Japanese Architecture of the Momoyama Period*, Tokyo, 1962, Tuttle

KISHIDA, HIDETO. *Japanese Architecture*, Tokyo, 1959, Japan Travel Bureau

PAIN, ROBERT TREAT and ALEXANDER SCOPER. *The Art and Architecture of Japan*, Middlesex, 1955, Penguin Books Ltd.

SADDLER, A. L. *A Short History of Japanese Architecture*, Tokyo, 1962, Tuttle

SEIKE, KIYOSHI and CHARLES S. TERRY. *Contemporary Japanese House*, Tokyo, 1964, Kodansha International

SUZUKI, DAISETSU. *Zen and Japanese Culture*, Tokyo, 1941, Iwanami Publishing Co.

TANGE, KENZŌ. "Structural Composition of Modern Architecture and Tradition of Japanese Architecture," *Japan Architect*, June 1956, Tokyo, Shin Kenchiku-sha

TANGE, KENZŌ and NOBORU KAWAZOE. *Ise: Prototype of Japanese Architecture*, Cambridge, 1965, the M.I.T. Press

TAUT, BRUNO. *Houses and People of Japan*, Tokyo, 1937, Sanseido

WATSUJI, TETSURŌ. *A Climate—A Philosophical Study*, Tokyo, 1964, Japanese UNESCO

IN JAPANESE

ENDŌ, MOTOO and OTHERS, eds. *Nihon Rekishi Series* (The Japanese History Series), 22 Vols. Tokyo, 1966, 1967, Sekai Bunka-sha

FUJIWARA, GIICHI. *Shoin-zukuri no Kenkyū* (Research on the Shoin Style), Kyoto, 1946, Takagiri Shuppan-sha

GROPIUS, WALTER, KENZŌ TANGE, and YASUHIRO ISHIMOTO. *Katsura; Nihon Kenchiku ni okeru Dentō to Sōzō* (Katsura, Tradition and Creation in Japanese Architecture), Tokyo, 1960, Zōkei-sha

INOUE, TAKEO. *Nihon Tanjō no Nazo* (The Riddle of the Birth of Japan), Tokyo, 1964, Kōdan-sha

ITŌ, TEIJI. *Nihon Design Ron* (A Theory of Japanese Design), Tokyo, 1966, Kajima Shuppan-kai

ITŌ, TEIJI and TAKEJI IWAMIYA. *Kekkai no Bi* (The Beauty of the *Kekkai*), Tokyo, 1966, Tankō-shin-sha

ITŌ, TEIJI and YUKIO FUTAGAWA. *Nihon no Minka* (The Japanese Farmhouse), Tokyo, 1960, Bijutsu Shuppan-sha

IWAMIYA, TAKEJI. *Katachi; Nihon no Denshō* (Katachi; A Picture-book of Traditional Japanese Workmanship), 2 Vols, Tokyo, 1962, Bijutsu Shuppan-sha

KAWAZOE, NOBORU. *Tami to Kami no Sumai* (Residences of Man and the Gods), Tokyo, 1963, Kōbun-sha

KITAO, HARUMICHI. *Chasitsu Kenchiku* (Tea House Architecture), Tokyo, 1956, Shōkoku-sha

KON, WAJIRŌ. *Nihon no Minka* (The Farmhouses of Japan), Tokyo, 1954, Sagami-shobō

NIHON BUNKA FORUM, eds. *Nihon Bunka no Dentō to Hensen* (Tradition and Transition in Japanese Culture), Tokyo, 1958, Shinchō-sha

NIHON KENCHIKU GAKKAI, eds. *Nihon Kenchiku-shi Zushū* (A History of Japanese Architecture (charts)), Tokyo, 1964, Shōkoku-sha

NIHON KENCHIKU KYŌKAI, eds. *Furusato no Sumai* (Hometown Houses), Osaka, 1962, Nihon Kenchiku Kyōkai

ŌTA, HIROTARŌ. *Nihon Kenchiku-shi Josetsu* (Introduction to the History of Japanese Architecture), Tokyo, 1962, Shōkoku-sha

SEKINO, MASARU. *Nihon Jūtaku Shōshi* (A Brief History of the Japanese House), Tokyo, 1942, Sagami-shobō

SHINOHARA, KAZUO. *Jūtaku Kenchiku* (Residential Architecture), Tokyo, 1966, Kinokuniya Shoten

TANGE, KENZŌ, NOBORU KAWAZOE and YOSHIO WATANABE. *Ise; Nihon Kenchiku no Genkei* (Ise; Prototype of Japanese Architecture), Tokyo, 1962, Asahi Shinbun-sha

GLOSSARY

Ajiro–thin strips of bamboo or wood woven together to form a wicker-work covering for sliding partitions, walls, or ceilings.

Akamatsu–the Japanese red pine (*Pinus densiflora*).

Amado–a wooden sliding door usually stored in a compartment called a *tobukuro* and pulled out to cover the outside of the openings of a house for protection against rain, cold, or wind.

Arakabe–the under coats of clay on a Japanese wall in contrast to the finishing coats, or *shiage-kabe*.

Azekura–a building style used in storehouses. Logs cut to multi-sided sections are piled up in a way somewhat similar to that used in log cabins.

Cha-no-ma–the room in a Japanese house that doubles as living and dining room and in which people also sometimes sleep.

Chigaidana–an arrangement of ornamental shelves used at the side of *tokonoma* in *shoin*-style rooms.

Daikoku–a Japanese form of the Buddhist Mahākala mGon-dkar, though as Daikoku the god of wealth he appears as one of the Seven Gods of Good Fortune in a form totally unlike his earlier counterpart.

Daikoku-bashira–a particularly thick post almost in the dead center of certain houses. It seems to be connected in the Japanese mind both with the ancient *shin-no-mihashira* and with Daikoku, the god of wealth, who lends it his name.

Engawa–a board-floored veranda-like area under the eaves which runs along the side of *tatami*-floored rooms. It is usually fitted with glass doors, *shoji*, or rain shutters on the outside.

Fuseki–what Teiji Itō calls the trump stone, the *fuseki* are actually the key elements in the plan of stepping stones.

Fusuma–a sliding partition made of a wooden lattice framework covered with paper or cloth.

Futon–the Japanese bed, consisting of a thick mattress-like under-layer with quilts on top for warmth.

Gasshō–a roof style found in the mountainous parts of the country. Unlike most Japanese roof structures, the *gasshō* uses diagonal members arranged to form a steep peak.

Genkan–the entrance hall.

Go–a very popular game said by some to have come originally from India into China and by others to have originated in China 3,000 years ago. It is played with round black and white stones on a board marked off in small squares.

Gyō–moderately formal of the three styles used in calligraphy.

Hachō–a Japanese aesthetic principle involving harmony within discord.

Haniwa–clay cylinders and representations of humans, animals, and many other objects used in the burial mounds of the Period of the Tumuli (250–552 A.D.).

Hibachi–a charcoal brazier used for what limited amount of warmth it will give.

Hinoki–Japanese cypress (*Chamaecyparus obtusa*).

Hiwada-buki–cypress bark shingling used on roofs.

Hōnen Shōnin scrolls–a set of 48 scrolls painted in the early fourteenth century depicting the life of the famous priest Hōnen, the founder of the Jōdo sect. In the Chion-in in Kyōto.

Hon-gawara–the older of Japan's two methods of laying roofing tiles. It is similar in form to mission tiles.

Ishimusubi–a fist-size stone tied with cords and set on paths or stepping stones to indicate the direction guests at tea ceremonies are *not* to take in their walk through the garden.

Jō–a reading of the Chinese character used for *tatami* mats. Floor space is almost always measured in terms of *jō*.

Jōdan-no-ma–an elevated section in one end of a formal *shoin* room.

271

From this raised area the master of the household would conduct receptions.

Kami–the Japanese word for spirit or god.

Kamoi–a lintel into which sliding partitions fit.

Kara-kusa–a stylized folliage pattern; when applied to tiles, the word means the cross section of pan tiles used in the *nihon-gawara* style. A line of such tiles seen from the eaves end resembles the *kara-kusa* ornamental pattern.

Kasō–important aspects of a house often determined by divination.

Kekkai–in the sense used in this book, a barrier used to separate the inner and outer sections of a temple, and later used in domestic architecture to indicate an area set apart for a special purpose, i.e., financial reckoning.

Ken–unit of linear measurement–six *shaku*, or just under six feet.

Kichō–a space divider used in ancient buildings and consisting of a framework from which hung silken draperies.

Kirizuma–a gabled roof.

Kiwari–traditional modular system of measurements.

Kokera-buki–shingle roofing.

Kōshi-do–a lattice door of wood or bamboo.

Kotatsu–originally, a sunken hearth with a heavily covered table over it around which the family sat, feet down in the hearth for warmth. Modern *kotatsu* are low tables fitted with heat lamps.

Kuni–the word used generally now to indicate a nation, though actually referring to a district or a segment of land under a single government, i.e. ancient Japanese *kuni* or provinces.

Ma–a Japanese word usually translated "room," though actually a much less closely limited space than the English word implies.

Mairado–a door made of an outer frame with slender horizontal crosspieces and filled with thin boards.

Musō-mado–a lattice window with one set of fixed boards as far apart as they are wide and another set of movable boards of the same width set in another track. By pulling the movable lattice in one direction it is possible to close the window entirely. Pushing it the other arranges the two sets of boards one directly on top of the other so that openings occur and air and light can pass through.

Naga-hibachi–a copper-lined brazier set into a low wooden cabinet which usually has draws down one side.

Nageshi–a horizontal member attached on the outer surfaces of the columns in a room.

Naka-nuri–the middle coat of clay in a Japanese wall.

Namako–a wall with tiles set into plaster. The plaster among the tiles is usually high and rounded.

Nekoma–a smaller removable inset panel in *shōji*.

Nenjū Gyōji scrolls–originally 60 scrolls depicting annual ceremonies. Unfortunately the few scrolls remaining today are copies of the twelfth-century originals.

Nihon-gawara–the later system of tile roofing which uses pan tiles.

Norito–an incantation used in Shinto ceremonies.

Ōkabe–stud wall finished on both sides.

Okidatami–rush mats placed on the board floors of ancient houses according to the time and the need.

Ōkuninushi-no-mikoto–a primitive Japanese deity to whom the Great Izumo Shrine is dedicated.

Okuzashiki–the innermost and most formal sitting room.

Oni-gawara–an ornamental finial tile originally patterned after the face of a demon, hence *oni* (demon) *kawara* (tile).

Oshi-ire–a Japanese-style closet.

Rei–soul or spirit.

Sabi–one of the famous elements, along with *wabi*, of *shibusa*, the Japanese aesthetic of semi-rustic refinement and beauty in the simple, and faintly melancholy.

Sakaki–the holy Shinto tree, (*Cleyera ochnacea*).

Sarariman–salary-man or white-collar worker.

Seiden–the main building in a complex of buildings, used in this book in connection with the *shinden*-style mansion.

Shaku–a traditional unit of measurement, just under one foot.

Shide–folded paper ritual ornaments used in Shinto practice.

Shigisan *Engi* scrolls–a humorous set of three scrolls dating from the second half of the twelfth century and now the property of the Chō-gosonshi-ji temple.

Shikkui–a Japanese plaster.

Shimenawa–a Shinto ritual straw rope used generally to mark of a sacred zone.

Shin–the most formal of the three styles used in calligraphy.

Shinden–an ancient mansion style featuring gardens, a pond, a main section which faced south, and numerous other out buildings all connected by means of covered walkways.

Shin-gyō-sō–the three style of writing Chinese characters, the first the most formal, the second moderately formal, and the third informal.

Shin'iki–holy precincts, as of a shrine.

Shin-kabe–the Japanese-style wall, in which the columns are exposed.

Shin-no-mihashira–the symbolic post under the floor of the main hall of the Ise Shrine.

Shita-nuri–the bottom coat of clay in a Japanese wall.

Shitomido–an ancient lattice door in two sections. The upper section, attached to the top *nageshi*, was hinged and could be hung open from above. The lower section fitted into the bottom *nageshi* and could be removed entirely.

Shoin–a bay window with a writing shelf-desk originally found in priests homes and later the distinctive feature of the *shoin* residential style, to which it gave its name.

Shōji–light wooden lattices covered with rice paper and used as sliding partitions.

Sō–the least formal and imaginatively free of the calligraphy styles.

Sudare–bamboo blinds.

Sugi–Japanese cedar (*Cryptomeria japonica*).

Sukiya–an architectural style greatly influenced by the tea house.

Sumi–Chinese black ink.

Sumitsubo–a wooden container for Chinese black ink and string which carpenters use in drawing lines.

Ta–see *ta-no-ji-gata*.

Taian–lucky days, useful in divination.

Tai-no-ya–the out buildings in a *shinden* mansion.

Taka-yuka–elevated floor, as in the ancient pile-house.

Tan–the fixed length of a roll of cloth for use in kimono or *futon*, (about 12 yards).

Ta-no-ji-gata–a farmhouse style laid out in the shape of the letter *ta*, 田.

Tansu–a traditional Japanese chest of drawers.

Tatami–straw and rush mats used for flooring in traditional Japanese houses.

Tate-ana–ancient pit-dwelling.

Tate-mae–the ceremony held when the house structure goes up.

Ten-chi-jin–the heaven-earth-man principle which Teiji Itō calls the aesthetic triangle.

Tobukuro–compartments built beside openings to hold the *amado*, or rain shutter doors.

Tokobashira–the non-structural post beside a *tokonoma* alcove.

Tokonoma–an ornamental alcove.

Tsubo–a unit of land measure, (about 4 square yards).

Tsuridono–a fishing pavilion in a *shinden* mansion, usually at the end of a long covered walkway.

Tsuri-ki–vertical members supporting a Japanese ceiling by linking it to the strut structure above.

Uwanuri–the top or finishing coat of clay in a Japanese wall.

Wabi–see *sabi*.

Wa-goya–the Japanese roof truss system.

Yakumono–the key elements in garden design, including the *yakuseki* or key stone, the *yakueda*, or key branch, and the *yakumoku*, or key tree.

Yani-matsu–a resinous pine.

Yosemune–a hipped roof.

Zabuton–square cushions used for sitting on the *tatami*.

Zashiki–the sitting room, usually a well appointed room in which one receives guests.

Zōri–Japanese thonged sandals.

INDEX

NOTE: *Numbers in italics indicate pages on which illustrations appear.*